The French Theater of the Absurd

Twayne's World Authors Series
French Literature

David O'Connell, Editor
Georgia State University

TWAS 822

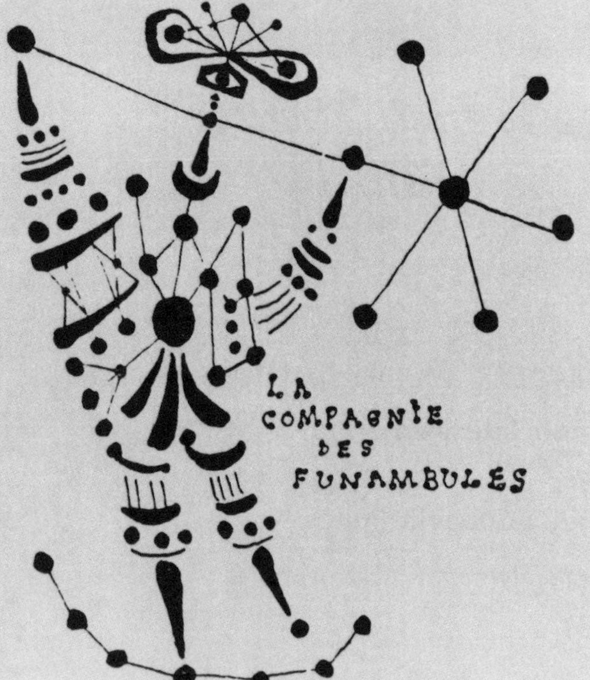

Program cover design by Jacques Noël for the Théâtre du Nouveau Lancry. Reprinted by permission of Jacques Noël and the Délégation à l'action artistique de la ville de Paris.

The French Theater of the Absurd

Deborah B. Gaensbauer

Regis College

Twayne Publishers
A Division of G. K. Hall & Co. • Boston

The French Theater of the Absurd
Deborah B. Gaensbauer

Published by Twayne Publishers
A division of G. K. Hall & Co.
70 Lincoln Street
Boston, Massachusetts 02111

Copyediting supervised by Barbara Sutton.
Book production by Janet Z. Reynolds.
Book design by Barbara Anderson.
Typeset by Graphic Sciences Corp., Cedar Rapids, Iowa.

10 9 8 7 6 5 4 3 2 1

The paper used in this publication meets the minimum requirements of American National Standard for Information Sciences—Permanence of Paper for Printed Library Materials, ANSI Z39.48-1984. ♾™

Printed and bound in the United States of America.

Library of Congress Cataloging-in-Publication Data

Gaensbauer, Deborah B.
The French theater of the absurd / Deborah B. Gaensbauer.
p. cm — (Twayne's world authors series ; TWAS 822. French literature)
Includes bibliographical references (p.) and index.
ISBN 0-8057-8270-2
1. French drama—20th century—History and criticism. 2. Theater of the absurd—History. I. Title. II. Series: Twayne's world authors series ; TWAS 822. III. Series: Twayne's world authors series. French literature.
PQ558.G34 1991
842′.91409—dc20 91-17614

To Ted, John, and James

Contents

Preface

The French theater of the absurd encompasses a broad spectrum of plays by very diverse playwrights, who have challenged directors' and spectators' notions of what an evening in the theater should be for nearly half a century. In this study, I have concentrated on works that were written by that movement's best-known playwrights during the 1950s and 1960s, the years when they were most spontaneously innovative. In my discussion of these plays I have attempted to bring them to life as texts meant for *performance.* One of the problems with reading plays or reading about plays is that it is often difficult to keep in mind that theater is, above all else, a physical event meant to be seen on a stage. This is especially true for the theater of the absurd, where the most revolutionary messages were less often conveyed by words themselves than by the astounding manner and physical contexts in which those words were delivered and received. Drawing on directors' notes and newspaper reviews of early performances, I have also tried to capture the critical reception that initially greeted these plays, hoping to make clear for today's audiences and readers, who have come to expect the kind of license with language and staging introduced by the absurdist playwrights, just how revolutionary their approach to the theater was.

All of the major dramatic works by Samuel Beckett and Jean Genet are presented here; most of Eugène Ionesco's are discussed. For Arthur Adamov and Fernando Arrabal, who were involved with the theater of the absurd early in their careers but experimented with other kinds of theater later, only representative plays are examined. A chapter on earlier literary movements to which the absurdist playwrights had strong ties, and one on the influential dramatic concepts of Antonin Artaud, precede the discussions of Beckett, Ionesco, Adamov, Genet, and Arrabal. A brief look at the performance-based theater that developed in the late 1960s and 1970s, owing a great debt to the innovations of the theater of the absurd, concludes the study.

Acknowledgments

I thank Grove Press for permission to quote from works by Artaud, Beckett, Ionesco, Adamov, Genet, and Arrabal; Georges Borchardt, Inc., for permission to quote from *Modern French Theater*; and the Délégation à l'action artistique de la ville de Paris for permission to quote from *Petites Scènes, grand théâtre*. I am particularly grateful to Jacques Noël for permission to reproduce his design for a theater program as the frontispiece. Portions of chapter 6 appeared in altered form in *Modern Drama* 28, no. 3; I thank the editors for permission to reprint. To my colleagues Roger Martin and Margaret McDonald, and to Andrea Watson, and to Dominique Akoka I wish to extend a special thanks for their invaluable assistance and encouragement.

Chronology

1896 Antonin Artaud born in Marseilles. *Ubu Roi* performed in Paris.

1906 Samuel Beckett born in Foxrock, Dublin.

1908 Arthur Adamov born in Kislovodsk, Russia.

1910 Jean Genet born in Paris.

1912 Eugène Ionesco born in Slatina, Romania.

1914 Dada movement founded in Zurich.

1924 André Breton publishes the first *Manifesto of Surrealism.*

1926 Artaud founds Alfred Jarry Theater with Roger Vitrac and Robert Aron.

1932 Fernando Arrabal born in Melilla, Spanish Morocco.

1935 Artaud founds Theater of Cruelty.

1938 Artaud's *The Theater and Its Double* published.

1947 Genet's *The Maids* performed in Paris.

1948 Antonin Artaud dies.

1949 Genet's *Deathwatch* performed in Paris.

1950 Ionesco's *The Bald Soprano* performed in Paris. Adamov's *The Great and the Small Maneuver* performed in Paris.

1951 Ionesco's *The Lesson* performed in Paris.

1952 Ionesco's *The Chairs* performed in Paris. Adamov's *The Parody* performed in Paris.

1953 Beckett's *Waiting for Godot* performed in Paris. Adamov's *Professor Taranne* performed in Lyon. Ionesco's *Victims of Duty* performed in Paris.

1954 Ionesco's *Amédée; or, How to Get Rid of It* performed in Paris.

1955 Ionesco's *Jack; or, The Submission* performed in Paris. Adamov's *Ping-Pong* performed in Paris.

1956 Genet's *The Balcony* performed in London.

1957 Beckett's *Endgame* performed in London.

1958 Beckett's *Krapp's Last Tape* performed in London.

1959 Genet's *The Blacks* performed in Paris. Beckett's *Happy Days* performed in New York. Arrabal's *Picnic on the Battlefield* performed in Paris.

1960 Ionesco's *Rhinoceros* performed in Paris.

1962 Ionesco's *Exit the King* performed in Paris.

1966 Genet's *The Screens* performed in Paris. Ionesco's *Hunger and Thirst* performed in Paris at the Comédie-Française. Arrabal's *The Car Cemetery* performed in Dijon.

1967 Arrabal's *The Architect and the Emperor of Assyria* performed in Paris. Arrabal imprisoned in Spain for blasphemous inscription.

1969 Arrabal's *And They Put Handcuffs on the Flowers* performed in Paris. Beckett awarded the Nobel Prize in literature.

1970 Arthur Adamov dies. Ionesco elected to the Académie française.

1971 Mnouchkine's *1789* performed in Vincennes.

1986 Jean Genet dies.

1989 Samuel Beckett dies.

Introduction

The term *theater of the absurd* was coined in 1961 by Martin Esslin, then a drama critic for the BBC. He used it as the title for a book focused on the unconventional, antirational plays of Samuel Beckett, Arthur Adamov, Eugène Ionesco, Jean Genet, and the British dramatist Harold Pinter, with brief descriptions of several lesser-known playwrights writing in a similarly illogical style.[1] Although only one of the five major figures discussed by Esslin, Jean Genet, was a native Frenchman, the theater of the absurd in its early stages was very much a French, more precisely a Parisian, phenomenon. Adamov, originally from Russia, and Ionesco, born in Romania, lived in Paris and wrote in French. Beckett was Irish, but he, too, lived in Paris and wrote his first plays in French. The first performances of most of their plays were given in little theaters in Paris.

The era of the French theater of the absurd stretches roughly across two decades, from 1948 to 1968. In 1948 Adamov's first play, *The Parody,* was in rehearsal, and Eugène Ionesco discovered the English grammar manual that was to inspire *The Bald Soprano.* Samuel Beckett began writing *Waiting for Godot* in the winter of 1948. That same year the death of Antonin Artaud, a poet and theater visionary, focused attention on his revolutionary notions of theater, many of which were incorporated in the theater of the absurd. By 1968 Genet had stopped writing plays and was in the United States collaborating with the Black Panthers. Adamov wrote his last complete play that year. Beckett and Ionesco were still writing, but without the irreverent spontaneity of their early theater. In 1969 Beckett was awarded the Nobel Prize in literature. A year later Ionesco became a member of the conservative Académie française. Ascension to the ranks of the "Immortals," as academy members are known, effectively constituted dismissal from the avant-garde. Nineteen sixty-eight was also the year when student radicals occupied the prestigious Odéon Theater in Paris. For a few weeks, the Odéon became a forum for improvised performances, ideological debates, and carnavalesque events, a spontaneous example of the politicized performance-based spectacles that were replacing the theater of the absurd as the in vogue experimental French theater.

It was not a concerted literary movement. Beckett, Ionesco, Adamov, and Genet began writing for the theater at the same time and worked with many of the same actors and directors, but their styles were eclectic, and for the most part they kept a respectful distance from one another. Their names have been linked since the early 1950s, however, because, at a time when spoken language was losing its power to persuade or shock, they recognized the truth of Artaud's claim that "the stage is a concrete physical place which asks to be filled, and to be given its own concrete language to speak."[2] Each was determined to undermine the purposes and methods of the traditional French theater, whether that tradition was represented by successful recipes for boulevard theater (the equivalent of Broadway shows in the United States) or the philosophical dramas of Albert Camus and Jean-Paul Sartre, which were at their peak of popularity when Adamov, Ionesco, Beckett, and Genet first began writing plays. They revolutionized the stage with an emphatically physical theater drawn from private obsessions, experiences of exile and alienation, dreams, and absolute disregard for conventional literary language.

The theater of the absurd is antirealistic, antipsychological, antiphilosophical, and apolitical. Plots, individual identities, comprehensible human relationships, plausible settings, and rational language are bafflingly, sometimes even terrifyingly, absent. In their place are ambiguous, repetitive, nightmarish situations involving alienated, mechanical characters whose clowning nullity is emphasized by childish, vague, or punning names. The language in these plays is pointedly unrealistic, a derisive combination of poetry and profanity, with a deflating humor of distorted aphorisms, clichés, and non sequiturs. Unlike the naturalist theater, which attempts to maintain an illusion of reality, the theater of the absurd is insistently ceremonial and theatrical. It blatantly imitates the excesses of the circus, vaudeville, and melodramas or parodies the great tragedies in the Western literary canon and even sacred rites, turning them into grotesquely humorous distortions of everyday life. Nevertheless, real life is what this theater is about. As Peter Brook, a well-known director whose early style was influenced by these plays, observed, "The theatre of the Absurd did not seek the unreal for its own sake. It used the unreal to make certain explorations because it sensed the absence of truth in our everyday exchanges, and the presence of truth in the seemingly far-fetched."[3]

Like the French New Novel, which came into being in the 1950s and simultaneously liberated literature from ideology, psychology, linear plots, and dialogues constructed with artificial coherency, the theater of the absurd is very much a phenomenon of the postwar years. The prevailing mood of the era is captured in the title that New Novelist Nathalie Sarraute gave to a ground-breaking volume of literary criticism in 1953: *The Age of Suspicion.*

Among the events that shaped both the theater of the absurd and the New Novel were the development of the hydrogen bomb; the return to a smug bourgeois complacency that marked the economic recovery of the De Gaulle era; the violent repression by French forces of the revolt in Algeria; and distrust of the hegemony of the United States coupled with a growing disillusion with the Soviet Union. In contrast to the concrete, heroic struggles and ideals of the Resistance years in France, the early years of the cold war spawned political passivity, generalized anger, and a mounting sense of alienation. The theater of the absurd expressed a very personal but widely shared anguish and seemingly incurable ennui. In 1946 Adamov wrote in his *Confession,* "All I know of myself is that I suffer. And if I suffer, it is because at the origin of myself there is mutilation, separation."[4] His first plays are exorcistic depictions of this existential mutilation. In Beckett's *Waiting for Godot,* perhaps the most painfully beautiful exposure of the raw nerves of absurd man ever written, Estragon observes, "Nothing happens, no one comes, no one goes, it's terrible."[5] Few of these ominously comical plays enjoyed a long first run. The clowns and nameless derelicts; the hallucinatory and inconsequential dialogues; the total disregard for the logic of plot, time, space, and sequential language; the bare-bones staging—all of these incensed spectators who had grander expectations for the theater. Critical attention, with a very few perceptive exceptions, was negative. In 1950 the reviewer for a conservative Paris newspaper claimed, after seeing a performance of Ionesco's *The Bald Soprano,* that the actors were doing theater a disservice by performing it.[6]

The term *theater of the absurd* has never been universally accepted. French critics generally refer to these plays as *nouveau théâtre* (new theater). Other labels proposed include theater of derision, theater of cruelty, avant-garde, antitheater, and metatheater. Esslin chose the name because he found in these plays a metaphysical anguish very similar to the concept of the absurd described by Camus. In the introduction to *The Theatre of the Absurd,* he cites Camus's *The Myth of Sisyphus* to illustrate the kind of alienation that is fundamental to the plays he is about to examine: "'A world that can be explained by reasoning, however faulty, is a familiar world. But in a universe that is suddenly deprived of illusions and light, man feels a stranger. His is an irremediable exile, because he is deprived of memories of a lost homeland as much as he lacks the hope of a promised land to come. This divorce between man and his life, the actor and his setting, truly constitutes the feeling of Absurdity'" (Esslin, 23).

The absurdist playwrights were contemporaries of Sartre and Camus. Beckett was born in 1906, just a year after Sartre; Adamov in 1908;

Genet in 1910; and Ionesco in 1912, one year before Camus. As young men they had been scarred by the same deplorable events: "The Moscow trials, the dictatorship of Stalin crushing all dissenters, the ascent of Hitler rallying thousands of German professors, writers, scientists, pastors around him, the self-deception of the Western democracies refusing to concede the obvious, then the outbreak of another war and, in France, the collapse of the ruling and presumably intelligent, classes in 1940, all that reinforced the conviction that absurdity was ruling unchallenged in Europe."[7] In this context Sartre—influenced by Søren Kierkegaard's concept of the absurd, Friedrich Nietzsche's pronouncement that "God is dead," the new approaches to consciousness and ethics of the phenomenologists, and Marxism—created his philosophical portraits of man as utterly alone, insignificant, and fettered with an unwelcome freedom in a world with no absolute values, a situation rendered all the more scandalously absurd by the knowledge that he is condemned to die. Voicing a similar anguish, Camus reached a receptive audience in the 1940s and 1950s with his portraits of human beings yearning for answers about the meaning of existence but greeted only by silence and death. The absurdist theater reflects a similarly gloomy perspective. Ionesco described himself as "surrounded by the halo of creation, unable to embrace these insubstantial shades, lost to understanding, out of my element, cut off from something undefinable without which everything spells deprivation."[8] It was a sensation shared by the other absurdist playwrights. Nonetheless, although the angst the playwrights expressed was nourished by many of the same fears and deceptions that moved Sartre and Camus, its treatment was markedly different.

For Sartre and Camus, recognition of the absurd was not an end in itself but a springboard to a unique concept of freedom and from there to political engagement. Camus compared modern man to Sisyphus and concluded that in spite of his miserable situation he must be happy because "there is no fate that cannot be surmounted by scorn."[9] The issue of responsibility, however, is not one that surfaces among the many challenges of the theater of the absurd, whose creators were more profoundly culturally alienated and who began writing for the theater in their late thirties and forties, bereft of any youthful illusions. The theater of the absurd is a theater of stasis and defeat in which the theme of death is omnipresent. It depicts an unshakable kind of alienation that does not lend itself to an intellectualized response. The theater of the absurd is not primarily a theater of dialogue and ideas but an immediate, gut-level, physical rendering of rejection, isolation, and futility. It is closer to August Strindberg's earlier experiments with dream theater and to the disillusioned bitter comedy and the questioning of truth and reality found in the plays of Luigi Pirandello and in Franz Kafka's depictions of nightmarish, immobilizing guilt and frustration. There is much humor but little joy in the absurdist plays.

Both the existentialists and the absurdists belonged to a generation of writers suspicious of a language that had been worn out in slogans, propaganda, and jargon. Nevertheless, Sartre and Camus maintained a certain faith in the possibility of rational discourse. Sartre, who wrote that he distrusted the incommunicable as "the source of all violence," insisted that "if words are sick, it is up to us to cure them."[10] The absurdist playwrights reacted very differently. The new language that they wanted to create for the stage was not one in which words would be cured but one that would be "cured" of words. Early in his career Beckett had expressed a desire "to bore one hole after another in [language], until what lurks behind it—be it something or nothing—begins to seep through."[11] At the time when Esslin chose the landmark title for his book about the new theater of the 1950s, the vogue of existentialism and Camus's notion of the absurd made it an apt and felicitous choice. At a distance of three decades from the once almost overwhelming influence of Sartre and Camus, however, it seems increasingly clear that the main roots of this revolutionary drama are not in the philosophical and political debates of the 1940s. The theater of the absurd is the culmination of a linguistic revolt that began in France in the middle of the nineteenth century and turned into a full-fledged subversive literary movement in the twentieth with the advent of Dada and surrealism.[12]

Part 1.
Antecedents

Chapter One

Jarry, the Dadaists, and the Surrealists

Nineteenth-Century Roots

Flaubert and the Modernist Poets Early models for the theater of the absurd proliferated in France during the second half of the nineteenth century, a period when the fallout of mediocrity, boredom, and sordidness from the Industrial Revolution created what Jacques Barzun, in the introduction to his translation of Gustave Flaubert's *Dictionnaire des idées reçues* as *Dictionary of Accepted Ideas,* refers to as a "growing awareness of mass production in word and thought."[1] Flaubert (1821–80), acknowledged by the absurdist playwrights as one of their primary sources of inspiration, reacted with satirical venom to the cheapening of language and reason by an increasingly dominant bourgeois society. In his novels *Madame Bovary* (1857), *L'Éducation sentimentale* (1869; *Sentimental Education*), and *Bouvard et Pecuchet* (1881; *Bouvard and Pecuchet*), as in the astute inanities of his *Dictionary of Accepted Ideas,* he inflated the middle-class languages of love, literature, science, and reason with irony until they became grotesque ingredients of black farce.[2]

Flaubert's contemporary, Charles Baudelaire (1821–67), echoed his pessimism in poems depicting modern man as a lonely, neurotic urban exile, nostalgic for lost paradises and seeking artificial substitutes in opium and decadent eroticism. Baudelaire's observation in "Anywhere Out of This World" that "life is a hospital where each patient is obsessed by the desire to change beds," heralded the restless despair and ennui that characterize twentieth-century literature. Baudelaire countered the Philistinism he saw triumphant all around him by inventing a symbolic poetic language, evocative of realities and harmonies inaccessible to rational interpretations. It is to Baudelaire that the honor of initiating what is now called the modernist revolution is generally attributed. "Since Baudelaire," according to Matei Calinescu, who describes him as "an almost perfect example of the modern artist's alienation from the society and official culture of his age," the "aesthetics of modernity has been consistently an aesthetics of imagination, opposed to any kind of realism."[3]

Influenced by Baudelaire, the poets Stéphane Mallarmé (1842–98) and Arthur Rimbaud (1854–91) experimented even more radically with destructive private myths and alchemical languages as keys to unlocking the resources of unreason. Reflecting on the late nineteenth-century crisis of language, Iris Murdoch notes that "suddenly it seemed that the whole referential character of language had become . . . a sort of irritant or stumbling block." Mallarmé's response, according to Murdoch, was an attempt to make language "into a pure and non-referential structure on its own," whereas Rimbaud's was "to weaken the referential character of language by overloading it."[4] Rimbaud's tactic, the overloading of language, became one of the most powerful revolutionary tools of the twentieth century. As Baudelaire had done before him, Rimbaud looked for inspiration in provocative combinations of mystical visions, popular culture, and social taboos, and swung between blasphemy and a desperate nostalgia for a childlike innocence.

The ferocity of Rimbaud's attack on society and literature found simultaneous expression in the work of a young and equally histrionic contemporary of Rimbaud, the count of Lautréamont (a pseudonym for Isadore Ducasse [1846–70]). His mock-epic, *The Songs of Maldoror,* was first published in 1868 but did not become well known until it was discovered 50 years later by the surrealists who made its author their patron saint. Lautréamont carried the poetic exploitation of violence and evil and the sabotage of reason to even greater extremes than Rimbaud. In his "intermittent annihilation of human faculties" Lautréamont attempted to sweep away every remnant of civilization.[5] Maldoror announces that his project for mankind is to "rip the mask off his villainous muddy face and make the sublime falsehoods with which he deceives himself fall one by one, like balls of ivory into a silver bowl" (Lautréamont, 34). In the rebellious art and life of Rimbaud and Lautréamont are the seeds of Alfred Jarry's *Ubu,* the poetic savagery of Dada, and the defiant mysticism of surrealism, all of which would later shape the theater of the absurd.

Jarry's *Ubu Roi* and the Symbolist Stage At the end of the nineteenth century, under the spell of the symbolist poets and of composer Richard Wagner's concept of total theater, a *gesamtkunstwerk* blending music, plastic arts, dance, and dialogue, innovative French theater directors attempted to emancipate drama from the pseudo-scientific realism of the dominant naturalist theater. Reacting against the faith in reason that prevailed at the time, they inaugurated a symbolist theater where mystical language and dreamlike symbolic staging were meant to unleash irrational forces and to lead to the loftier truths of ideal realities. With the exception of the mysteriously static and silent dramas of the Belgian Maurice Maeterlinck (1862–1949), the symbolist theater was not a long-lived phenomenon. Nevertheless, from one end of the twentieth century to the other, the experimental French stage has been influenced by the symbolists' demonstration that dramatic language is more than dialogue and that the physical stage is not merely a frame or decoration but an essential signifying element of the theater.

It was an outrageous, skillful parody of symbolist theater, Albert Jarry's *Ubu Roi* (*Ubu the King*), that propelled French theater into the twentieth century. *Ubu,* which opened on 10 December 1896, with a resounding neologistic profanity, "merdre," permanently devalued dialogue and became a powerfully subversive model for twentieth-century playwrights. With *Ubu,* Rimbaud's proclamation that "now is the time of the ASSASSINS" came true in the theater. Aurélien Lugné-Poe, the young director who staged *Ubu,* had taken over a symbolist theater in 1893 and created the Théâtre de l'Oeuvre, where for the next 30 years he introduced Paris audiences to an extraordinary range of playwrights and stage innovations. Dedicated to making the theater a "work of art" and to "stirring up ideas," he experimented with lighting, color, movement, pantomime, and masks when he could afford to.[6] When funds were short, taking the Elizabethan stage as his model, he developed the suggestive potential of the bare stage. Jarry became Lugné-Poe's secretary in 1896 and used his position to promote *Ubu.* The antipsychological treatment of the characters in *Ubu* and Jarry's notions for a parodical, abstract staging naturally appealed to Lugné-Poe. Jarry called for a bare stage with a single minimal backdrop. Scene changes were to be indicated by actors carrying placards. Ubu was to be portrayed by an actor wearing a grotesque mask who would hang a horse's head from his neck for his equestrian scenes. Because Jarry found crowd scenes "an insult to the intelligence," he directed that the military parade and the battle scenes be represented by a single soldier. Costumes were to be stylized and anachronistic and the actors were to speak in unrealistic accents. When the curtain rose for the first performance, it revealed a set designed to represent "nowhere, with trees at the foot of beds and white snow in a summer sky." Appropriately, "the action takes place in Poland, a country so legendary, so dismembered that it is well qualified to be this particular Nowhere."[7]

Jarry's King Ubu is a Macbeth comically blown up in ego and avarice to gigantic proportions and reduced in intellect to a whining, cowardly moron.

Ubu begins with Ma Ubu persuading her astoundingly corpulent husband, once the king of Aragon but at present merely a captain of the king's dragoons, to murder the king of Poland. Become king, Ubu immediately betrays all his companions and destroys his noblemen, judges, and financiers, gleefully sending them through a trap door to his marvelous disembraining machine. He levies staggering taxes, perpetrates enormous carnage to collect them, and then goes off to fight the czar of Russia. Defeated, the Ubus flee by ship to Paris, where Ubu anticipates being appointed "Master of Phynances." En route, he takes over the captain's duties in the inimitable style that caused outraged spectators to start a brawl in the theater in 1896: "'Bout ship. Let go the anchor. Go about in stays, wear ship, hoist more sail, haul down sail, put the tiller hard over, up with the helm, full speed astern, give her more lee, splice the top gallant. How am I doing? Tight as a rivet! Meet the wave crosswise and everything will be shipshape. Avast there."[8]

In the Ubus' antics and warlike itinerary, audiences in 1896 could easily recognize the politics and social conflicts of France's Third Republic. Jarry held Ubu up to the audience as its mirror image: "Mr. Ubu is an ignoble creature, which is why he is so much like us all (seen from below)" (*SWAJ,* 80). The reflected image is that of a monstrous "slapstick puppet," as Ma Ubu calls her husband, who is infantile, cowardly, vulgar, and sadistic. This joyous slaughterer and plunderer, swearing by his green candle and asking, "Isn't injustice as good as justice," is also terribly funny as he travesties Rimbaud's "saison en enfer" (season in hell) with a descent into pure Freudian id.[9] Roger Shattuck has characterized Jarry's humor as "an enormous, unsparing thing."[10] The same can be said for Jarry's linguistic inventiveness. Ubu dismantles language and logic in a breathtaking series of neologisms, hyperboles, puns, blasphemies, and obscenities, made all the more outrageous by his schoolboyish enthusiasm and the pompous stylized manner of his delivery. For all its absurdity, the language in *Ubu* is also rich with a Rabelaisian zest and a tumbling poetry. Jarry's absolute scorn for traditional dialogue led André Breton to observe that after Jarry, "literature moves dangerously on a minefield."[11]

The Silent Cinema Although *Ubu*'s dramatic license made Jarry an instant hero in avant-garde artistic circles, few playwrights were ready to take up his lead. It was the influence not of a theater event but of the silent cinema, which was introduced at the end of the nineteenth century, that would most profoundly transform expectations for the modern theater. Touching increasingly diverse audiences with fantastic images, a kaleidoscopic treatment of time and space, new kinds of heroes, and an extraordinary comic sophistication, all without the crutch of the spoken word, silent cinema demonstrated that the most powerful theater language is not eloquent rhetoric but the language of gesture, rhythm, and silence. Many of the early cinema prodigies began their careers in music hall routines and vaudeville. They brought to cinema both the genial sense of timing that drives successful vaudeville acts and a heightened awareness of the potentially threatening absurdity of physical objects. Silent film also gave the world its most remarkable absurd hero, Charlie Chaplin as the "little tramp," shuffling from one cruelly comic adventure to another. Chaplin became an indelible image of the twentieth century: the trammeled, alienated little man who somehow hangs on.

The first film projected in Paris for a paying audience was shown at the Grand Café in 1895.[12] By the time World War I broke out, film had grown into a full-fledged international industry.[13] Interviewed in 1916 about the future of the theater, Guillaume Apollinaire (1880–1918), a poet and playwright who attempted to keep Jarry's anarchistic spirit alive on the stage, predicted that it would be the cinema that would achieve the great modern *gesamtkunstwerk.*[14] The theater of the absurd is a product of generations who drew on cinematic images and techniques in their very individualized approaches to that Wagnerian ideal.

Twentieth-Century Roots

Apollinaire The prologue to Apollinaire's experimental play, *Les Mamelles de Tirésias* (*The Breasts of Tiresias*), calls for the kind of total spectacle he admired in film: "Sounds gestures colors cries tumults / Music dancing acrobatics poetry painting / Choruses actions and multiple sets."[15] *Tiresias,* begun in 1903 and completed in 1917 after Apollinaire had returned from the front with a shell wound to his head that would shortly prove fatal, epitomizes the revolutionary approach to theater that was taking shape in the tumultuous opening decades of the century. In the first act, Thérèse, tired of being a woman and eager to "make war not children," denounces her husband's tyranny, grows a beard and mustache, and becomes a man as her breasts—red and white balloons attached by string—fly off. Popping the balloons with a cigarette lighter, she becomes Tiresias. In the second act Thérèse's husband, whom she has forcibly dressed in her clothes, announces with satisfaction that he has given birth to 40,049 children in one day. After much noise, punning, and clowning on stage, the play ends with Thérèse's return to her husband.

In spite of many Jarryesque touches—such as the launching of Thérèse's balloon-breasts; a moving, talking kiosk; representation of the entire population of Zanzibar by a single speechless person; unnatural delivery of lines shouted through a megaphone; and the lighting of the fortune-teller's brain (Thérèse in disguise) with an electric light bulb—*Tiresias* was not as provocative or shocking when it was staged in 1917 as Apollinaire had hoped. It was the revolutionary approach to the stage sketched in its preface and prologue that made it an important event in theater history. Observing that "when man wanted to imitate walking he created the wheel, which does not resemble a leg" (*MFT,* 56), Apollinaire offered an early definition of surrealism. He based his formula for a modern theater on the same principle: "After all, the stage is no more the life it represents than the wheel is a leg" (*MFT,* 59). Holding up *Tiresias* as an example of "the reasonable use of the improbable," Apollinaire proposed circuslike innovations that were to be increasingly incorporated into modern productions. It was intended for a circular theater with two stages: "One in the middle / The other like a ring around the spectators permitting / The full unfolding of our modern art" (*MFT,* 66). Balls were tossed at the spectators to break down the barrier between the stage and the audience.

Dada By the time Apollinaire completed *Tiresias,* the Dada movement, which flourished in Zurich from 1914 to 1918 and then in Paris from 1918 to 1922, was already making the notion of "reasonable use of the improbable" forever too timid for the modern stage. Launched by a polyglot group seeking refuge from the trenches in neutral Zurich, Dada was a protest against the institutions and ideologies that had betrayed humanity by luring it into World War I. The movement was heavily influenced by the German philosopher Friedrich Nietzsche (1844–90), who challenged what he perceived as a dying civilization to go "beyond good and evil" and to welcome cruelty and the drive to power as natural expressions of genius. This proposition unleashed an enormous wave of counter-culture creativity that eventually fed into such diversely revolutionary concepts as Freudian psychology, Strindbergian expressionism, surrealism, and existentialism.[16] The dadaists carried on Lautréamont's "intermittent annihilation of human faculties." Their intentions, set forth in the various manifestos of Tristan Tzara, a Romanian actor and poet who became their chief impresario, were wholeheartedly destructive.

Dada rejected reason. "Thought," Tzara claimed, "is made in the mouth."[17] It was spontaneous and visceral. Audiences at a Dada production risked more than verbal assault. Dada events in Paris were frequently staged at street corners, where outraged passersby would be drawn into "happenings" in which spectacular impropriety was generally the key note. Language—"pretty threadbare, and yet it alone fills the lives of most men"—was one of Dada's primary targets (*L,* 90). In Dada productions, words were used to exclude or assault rather than engage the audience. The spoken portions of the early Dada performances typically consisted of largely incomprehensible dialogues, phonetic or "noise" poems, and chanting, accompanied by imitations of African rhythms and music. The performers adopted wooden gaits and stilted speech and emphasized the unnaturalness of their linguistic activities with preposterous costumes. Staging was equally unrealistic and provocative.

The physical and verbal excesses in Tzara's plays prepared the way for the theater of the absurd. The humorously barbaric combination of clichés, nonsense, scatology, and repetitive sounds in his *La Première aventure céleste de M. Antipyrine* (*The First Celestial Adventure of Mr. Antipyrine*), written in 1920, created a hallucinatory atmosphere that anticipated Ionesco's early theater. In this play, Tzara, playing himself, forecast the spirit of the new theater of the 1950s: "We are circus managers and we whistle through the wind at the fairs, through the convents, brothels, theatres, realities, sentiments, restaurants, ohi, hoho, bangbang."[18] He dismissed, in favor of the art of children, "the great ambassadors of sentiment who exclaimed historically in chorus Psychology Psychology heehee Science Science Science Vive la France" (*DP,* 59). *The Gas Heart,* which Tzara wrote in 1921, portrays the kind of despair over the impossibility of communication that would later characterize the theater of the absurd. When Mouth, for example, asks Nose (the other characters are Ear, Neck, and Eyebrow), "You mean to say: 'despair gives you its explanation regarding its rates of exchange,'" Nose retorts: "I don't mean to say anything. A long time ago I put everything I had to say into a hatbox" (*DP,* 143).

When Tzara moved to Paris in 1920, his anarchy was eagerly embraced by the future surrealists. André Breton, who became the high priest of surrealism, Paul Eluard, Louis Aragon, Philippe Soupault, and others played roles in a number of Dada spectacles including the first production of *The Gas Heart.* There was always rivalry and personality conflict, however. As early as 1921, when the students at the Ecole des beaux-arts had gone in procession to throw Dada's coffin in the Seine, Breton and several other surrealists followed along.[19] In 1923 the rupture between Dada and surrealism became official when Breton and Eluard, by then seriously at odds with Tzara, broke up a second production of *The Gas Heart* by starting a violent brawl in the theater. The situation became so violent that Tzara was forced to call the police, a necessary but un-Dada-like gesture. Dada was dying out as a revolutionary movement in Paris anyway. Its outrages were becoming predictable and assimilable, a fate that would similarly push the theater of the absurd from its position as the avant-garde French theater four and a half decades later.

Surrealism Despite the split, the surrealists remained committed to fundamental aspects of the Dada revolt. They continued to promote disorder, intuition, and chance. They objected to psychology and realism in literature, and remained preoccupied with the breakdown of language. However, if they were as conscious as the dadaists of the inability of language in its current state to express anything profoundly new, or even profound, they were no longer satisfied with a purely destructive response. Surrealism broke from the nihilism of Dada. Discovering the unknown became more important than destroying old nemeses. The surrealists integrated the fantastic, the occult, the irrational forces of desire and dreams, and the imaginative freedom of children into the most ordinary situations, attempting to transcend mundane surface realities and arrive at a "surreality" where the powerful forces of the unconscious could be tapped. "Surrealism," Antonin Artaud wrote in 1926, "has never meant anything to me but a new kind of *magic*. The imagination, the dream, that whole intense liberation of the unconscious whose purpose it is to raise to the surface of the soul all that it is in the habit of keeping concealed, must necessarily introduce profound transformations in the scale of appearances, in the value of signification and the symbolism of the created."[20]

A combination of the destructive black humor and violent lyricism of Lautréamont, psychic automatism, dream language, and psychopathology provided the basic tools for the surrealists' linguistic experiments. Breton, who studied medicine before the war and was acquainted with Charcot's lectures on hysteria, had become an admirer of Freud's work on dreams and the unconscious. He proposed pathological conversations as a model for surrealism, citing as an example the following dialogue between a doctor and his patient:

Q. "How old are you?"
A. "You."
(*Echolalia.*)

Q. "What is your name?"
A. "Forty-five houses."
(*Ganser syndrome, or beside-the-point replies*)[21]

Breton welcomed psychic disturbances as situations where "the words, the images are only so many springboards for the mind of the listener" (*M*, 35).[22]

Although the surrealists had written and performed in many plays, Breton eventually rejected the theater because he considered it a commercial enterprise. He expelled from the movement its one "official" playwright, Roger Vitrac, whose *Victor, ou les enfants au pouvoir* (*Victor; or, The Children Take Charge*) is the only surrealist play to remain in contemporary repertories. *Victor,* a savagely comic critique of the abuse of language in bourgeois society, combines the destructive humor of Dada and a surrealistic attempt to use linguistic distortions to lead to more promising orders of reality. With the exception of the maid, when the adult characters speak "normally," they wallow in clichés and deceit. Victor, a six-foot-tall precocity who dies of disgust with the adult world on his ninth birthday, imitates this hostile, empty parentspeak when he admonishes his little friend Esther, "Leave me alone. Take care of your dolls. Lick your cats, love your neighbor as yourself and be a good girl until you're a good wife and a good mother."[23] In contrast, when Victor "speaks surrealist," as Henri Béhar so aptly puts it, the poetic play of his nonsense rips away the facade of convention and reveals truths that the adults do not want to hear.[24] *Victor,* which points the way to Ionesco's theater and that of Fernando Arrabal, a younger representative of the absurdist movement, is an affirmation of André Breton's contention that "language was given to man for surrealist use" (*M*, 32).

Vitrac's concrete rendering of the contradictory realities of dream language in *Victor* anticipates another key ingredient of the theater of the absurd. He outraged his first audiences with the inexplicable arrival in the midst of sordid revelations about Victor's father of an ethereal women named Ida Mortemart, whose exoticism is countered by a cruel affliction with gas. Ida Mortemart created the kind of physical shock effect cherished by the surrealists and later much sought after by the absurdist playwrights, who were equally determined to make their audiences uncomfortable. *Victor*'s premiere in 1928 was the last gasp of Artaud's controversial and unsuccessful Alfred Jarry Theater. There were only three performances. In 1962, when *Victor* was revived in Paris by Jean Anouilh, it was an enormous box office success, acclaimed by a public accustomed by the theater of the absurd to the childlike inconsistencies of oneiric language and staging and the scandalous, menacing humor inherited from surrealism.

Dada and surrealism touched all of the major figures of the French theater of the absurd. Adamov participated in surrealist gatherings. Beckett translated poems by French surrealists into English and wrote surrealist poetry himself. He owed his first successful theatrical connection to Tristan

Tzara, who introduced director Roger Blin to *Godot* and *Eleutheria*. Ionesco, whose first plays so enchanted the surrealists that they were reproduced in their publications, also wrote poetry influenced by surrealism early in his career. Arrabal briefly joined the post–World War II surrealist movement in Paris. Most of the seven categories of drama reflecting a surrealist approach described by Eric Sellin are incorporated to various degrees in the theater of the absurd, principally the "staging of dreams," "concretizing the nononeiric subconscious," "unexpected physical or chronological juxtapositions," "the unexpected or grotesque as theatrical ingredient," and "the apotheosis of sundry mundane objects."[25] Although there were relatively few formally staged Dada or surrealist productions, their humorous or dreamlike scenic and linguistic innovations, contempt for plot and character development, and mockery of conventional dramatic genres provided working theatrical models for the next 50 years.

Chapter Two

Antonin Artaud

The techniques of surrealism have been described as the most powerful mental explosives ever invented: "Like rockets, one can use them for fireworks, for war, or for the propulsion of fantastic machines beyond the earth's atmosphere. Thus the rockets of surrealism can serve as anything from a diversion for snobs to a devastating subversion, or even to open access to unexplored worlds."[1] Antonin Artaud turned this weapon on the conventional theater and transformed the means by which twentieth-century theater would explore new worlds. Artaud's almost inhumanly ambitious demands for the rebirth of the theater were largely ignored or dismissed during most of his lifetime. Few paid much attention when his remarkable collection of essays, *Le Théâtre et son double* (*The Theater and Its Double*), first appeared in 1938. A new edition in 1944, however, found a wider audience among a postwar generation as disenchanted with reason, psychologizing, and empty rhetoric and as eager to revolutionize the theater as Artaud. By midcentury, when the works of the absurdist playwrights were first reaching the stage, the young directors who had been influenced by Artaud were increasingly in a position to ignite a revolution. Within a short time, Artaud's vision of a cruel, physical theater, and his call for a renewal of the way theater "speaks," began to affect every element of dramatic production: playwrights, plays, actors, directors, stage effects, theater architecture, and audiences. Susan Sontag did not exaggerate when she declared in the introduction to Artaud's *Selected Works* that "he has had an impact so profound that the course of all recent serious theater in Western Europe and the Americas can be said to divide into two periods—before Artaud and after Artaud" (*SW,* xxxviii).

Background

Artaud's initiation into the theater as an actor was a determining factor in his intensely physical approach to the stage. In 1918 Artaud, whom a childhood bout with meningitis had left prone to terrible head pains and periods of depression that led to drug dependency and increasingly lengthy internments in psychiatric hospitals, was sent to a clinic just outside Paris. The director of the clinic introduced Artaud to Lugné-Poe, who offered him an acting job. Soon after, Artaud became associated with another brilliant director, Charles Dullin. Dullin, whose rejection of rhetoric and insistence on intuitive performance and simplicity of staging were revolutionizing the theater, captivated the young Artaud with his almost religious fervor and physical rigor: "It is all based on such a desire for moral *purity*. . . . We act with our heart of hearts, our hands, our feet, every muscle, every limb. We feel the object, we smell it, we touch it, we see it, we hear it—and there is nothing, there are no props."[2] Artaud also acted in a number of films. His gaunt, haunting face can still be seen in such masterpieces as Abel Gance's *Napoléon* (1926) and Carl Dreyer's *St. Joan* (1928). What he called the "unexpected and mysterious side" of silent cinema contributed to his conviction that "theater, like speech, needs to be set free" (*TD,* 118).

Artaud's dramatic vision was also heavily influenced by surrealism, a natural draw for someone who suffered from a psychic malady he described as a separation of self from words and images. His notion of an ideal theater echoes the surrealists' enthusiasm for oriental myths and rituals and also their faith in alchemical transformations of reality through the violent magic of poetry and dreams. "The theater will never find itself again, *i.e.,* constitute a means of true illusion," he maintained, "except by furnishing the spectator with the truthful precipitates of dreams, in which his taste for crime, his erotic obsessions, his savagery, his chimeras, his utopian sense of life and matter, even his cannibalism, pour out on a level not counterfeit and illusory, but interior" (*TD,* 92). Artaud did not share the surrealists' optimism, however. As Sontag notes, "The Surrealists are connoisseurs of joy, freedom and pleasure. Artaud is a connoisseur of despair and moral struggle" (*SW,* xxviii). He broke with the movement in 1926 when Breton and most of his group became members of the Communist party. Revolutionary to an extreme beyond politics, Artaud refused to join. Artaud's commitment to the theater and his association with Roger Vitrac, expelled earlier by Breton, were also important factors in the rupture.

Theater Experiments

Artaud had two opportunities to establish his own theater. In 1926, thanks largely to the generosity of the founder of the French Psychoanalytic Society, Dr. René Allendy, and his wife, Artaud, Roger Vitrac, and Robert Aron created the Alfred Jarry Theater. Artaud's manifestos for this theater reflect the influence of the symbolists, Jarry, and the surrealists. They also express intentions similar to those voiced by the absurdist playwrights more than two decades later. "We are not creating a theatre so as to present plays," he explained, "but to succeed in showing the mind's obscure, hidden and unrevealed aspects. . . . What we would like to see sparkle and triumph on stage is whatever is a part of the mystery and magnetic fascination of dreams, the dark layers of consciousness, all that obsesses us within our minds" (*CW,* 2:23). The Alfred Jarry Theater was aimed at such a thorough transformation of the spectator that Artaud compared it to a surgeon or a dentist. Not surprisingly, it was short-lived, closing in December 1928 with Vitrac's *Victor.*

In 1935 Artaud created his Theater of Cruelty, which failed even more rapidly, lasting only 17 days. Its single production was his version of *The Cenci,* a tale of incest, rape, and betrayal in sixteenth-century Italy, based on works by Shelley and Stendhal. Describing it to André Gide, he claimed that "there is *nothing* among the traditional notions of Society, order, Justice, Religion, family, and Country, that is not attacked" (*SW,* 340). Magnificent sets and costumes were created by Balthus, a painter associated with the surrealists. Unfortunately, the other resources available to Artaud were inadequate to his vision. Hastily assembled and underrehearsed actors played in an inappropriately large theater to an unreceptive audience and generally hostile critics. Completely discouraged, Artaud left France for Mexico to seek his ideal theater in the peyote rituals of the Tarahumaras Indians.

Revolutionary Vision

Artaud's legacy includes very few original dramatic works. *The Jet of Blood* (1925), his earliest play, is a rare example of a full text with complete stage directions by Artaud. Consisting of only four pages of printed text, it is nonetheless crowded with effects and events. In the opening lines, the action whirls from a lyric declaration of love between a brother and sister to their separation by a hurricane and a "crash of stars." At this moment the stage directions call for "a number of live pieces of human bodies falling down: hands, feet, scalps, masks, colonnades, porches, temples, and alembics, which, however, fall more and more slowly, as if they were falling in a vacuum. Three scorpions fall down, one after the other, and finally a frog and a beetle, which sets itself down with a maddening, vomit-inducing slowness" (*MFT,* 223). After the chaos, a Knight and a Nurse with enormous breasts, the mother and father of the young couple, appear, arguing viciously. In response to the Knight's demand, "Bitch let me eat," the Nurse gives him her breasts, which turn out to be a huge slice of Gruyère cheese. Shadowlike, a Priest, a Shoemaker, a cuckolded Sexton, a Whore, a Judge, and a Street Peddlar emerge. The Priest acknowledges that he is not much of a believer: "We others feed ourselves on the dirty little stories we hear in the confessional. And that's all there is—that's life" (*MFT,* 225). Night falls. There is another earthquake. Panicked, the characters run about in the kind of chaotic frenzy typical of slapstick films. Suddenly an enormous hand reaches out and grabs the Whore's hair, which catches fire. The Whore, whose dress has become transparent, revealing a hideous nude body, recognizes the hand of God and bites it. Blood from the wound spurts across the stage. The Nurse reappears with the young girl dead in her arms. The Knight whines to her for more cheese. In response, she lifts her skirt, releasing a swarm of scorpions that cover his genitals. Begging, "Don't hurt Mummy," in the voice of a ventriloquist's dummy, the young boy runs away with the nurse. The young girl revives to exclaim: "The virgin! Ah, that's what he was looking for" (*MFT,* 226). The curtain falls.

The startling and repulsive hallucinatory visual effects and the somewhat adolescent humor of the attack on all that society holds honorable or sacred are characteristic of Dada and surrealist productions. What is more specifically Artaudian in *Jet of Blood* is the intensity of the cruelty and depravity in a play that is both a blasphemy and a desperate poetic appeal for something still unsullied and powerfully symbolic in Western society. A similar destructive impulse, springing from a longing for a psychic wholeness and conceived in terms of symbolic and aesthetic purity, underlies the essays of *The Theater and Its Double* and explains in no small way Artaud's enduring appeal.

Unsuccessful in his "practical" theater endeavors, Artaud was finally able to impose his revolutionary visions as the author of *The Theater and Its Double.* The title was chosen because it "reflects all the doubles of theater I believe I have found over so many years, metaphysics, the plague, cruelty. . . . this word 'double' also refers to the great magical factor."[3] In these "doubles" Artaud sought a theater that would restore modern man to a primitive symbolic wholeness. Heavily influenced by Asian theater, Nietzsche's ideal Dionysian theater, and Lautréamont's *Maldoror,* Artaud believed that only a very physical, ritualized theater of unfettered cruelty would have the power to unmask secret instincts and desires and confront the spectator with meaningful symbols. Like the plague, true theater, according to Artaud, "restores . . . dormant conflicts and all their powers, and gives these powers names we hail as symbols . . . for there can be theater only from the moment when the impossible really begins and when the poetry which occurs on the stage sustains and superheats the realized symbols" (*TD,* 28). By cruelty, he did not mean standard stage violence (although there was plenty of it in his own work), nor did he mean poetic texts when he spoke of poetry. The cruel poetry envisioned by Artaud would arise from a new stage language, a ceremonial, physical language.

The ferocious laughter of Lautréamont, Jarry, Dada, and surrealism, which Artaud might have added to his list of "doubles," was to be an essential ingredient of this language of cruelty. His 1930 essay "The Alfred Jarry Theater and Public Hostility" calls for "*total laughter,* laughter extending from paralysed slavvering to convulsed, side-holding sobbing" (*CW,* 2:38). True theater, Artaud contends in "The Theater and the Plague," "disturbs the senses' repose, frees the repressed unconscious, incites a kind of virtual revolt . . . and imposes on the assembled collectivity an attitude that is both difficult and heroic" (*TD,* 27–28). The black humor in Artaud's ideal theater, which resurfaces as an essential ingredient of the theater of the absurd, has the same delirious communicative power as the plague and, like the plague, is both a purging and regenerative force. Artaud was wildly enthusiastic about the Marx brothers. His description of the end of *Monkey Business* extols its physical blend of humor and terror: "There is nothing at once so hallucinatory and so terrible as this type of man-hunt, this battle of rivals, this chase in the shadows of a cow barn, a stable draped in cobwebs, while men, women and animals break their bounds and land in the middle of a heap of crazy objects, each of whose *movements* or *noise* functions in its turn" (*TD,* 143).

Another of Artaud's notions that prefigures the theater of the absurd is that "theater will not be given its specific powers of action until it is given its language." Disdaining naturalist theater and "psychological" theater as his revolutionary predecessors had done, he considered theater to be a syncretic language creating "texts" with every aspect of the production: gesture, voice, lighting, costumes, accessories, sets, and architecture, as well as dialogue. When Artaud inaugurated his Alfred Jarry Theater, still strongly influenced by Charles Dullin, he called for a very spare staging and the elimination of "all those hateful trappings which clutter up a written play and turn it into a show, instead of it remaining within the limits of words, impressions and abstractions" (*CW,* 2:20). By the 1930s the discovery of the elaborate staging and ritual of the Balinese theater had enriched Artaud's vision and challenged him to examine the physical means by which "to link the theater to the expressive possibilities of forms, to everything in the domain of gestures, noises, colors, movements . . . to restore it to its original direction, to reinstate it in its religious and metaphysical aspect" (*TD,* 70). In the harmony of the ghosts and doubles in the Balinese theater and its stylized gestures and costumes, ritualized music, and archaic rhythms, he found his principal model for "a new physical language, based upon signs and no longer upon words" (*TD,* 54). A theater where speech was simply another physical object with a value and function equivalent to that of the other elements of the decor would be far superior, he believed, to the psychological theater of the Occident (*TD,* 89).

In a characteristic attack, he dismissed theater that does not give the primary role to its mise-en-scène as "theater of idiots, madmen, inverts, grammarians, grocers, antipoets and positivists, i.e., Occidentals" (*TD,* 41). The primary role assigned to mise-en-scène and the assumption that language must be used in "a concrete and spatial sense" implied a reversal of the relationship between director and author. One of the great appeals of the Balinese theater for Artaud was that the author's place is taken by a director who becomes "a kind of manager of magic, a master of sacred ceremonies" (*TD,* 60). In his "Letters on Language," Artaud wrote that if the theater is to survive, much less revive, it must "realize what differentiates it from text, pure speech, literature, and all other fixed and written means" (*TD,* 106). Insisting that the only one who has the right to call himself a creator in the theater is the one who controls the stage, Artaud proposed that the author also become a director to eliminate the "absurd duality" existing between them (*TD,* 112). Although for the playwrights of the absurd the text reigned supreme, they all worked very closely in making both textual and scenic changes with directors who had been strongly influenced by Artaud's ideas.[4] Beckett and Arrabal eventually did direct their own plays. The performance-based theater that sprang up in the 1960s and 1970s followed almost to the letter Artaud's notions of the premier role of the director and his suggestion in "Metaphysics and the *Mise en Scène*" that plays be composed directly on stage.

Artaud sought not only to transcend the "habitual boundaries of feelings and words" in the theater but also to transform the traditional physical boundaries of the stage. Among his most concrete proposals were recommendations for a theater architecture designed to "engulf" the spectator in the middle of the action, making it impossible to participate in the theater from a safe emotional or physical distance. He wanted to replace traditional theaters with empty halls, hangars, or barns where actor and spectator would occupy the same spaces. He also proposed the now familiar concept of connected galleries, permitting action and sound to move around the room and from one level to another, and the use of movable chairs, allowing an audience to follow the surrounding spectacle. Thus, according to Artaud, "just as there will be no unoccupied point in space, there will be neither respite nor vacancy in the spectator's mind or sensibility" (*TD,* 126).

By the time *The Theater and Its Double* appeared in print, Artaud's career in the theater was effectively over. After his return from Mexico in 1936, he was plagued by poverty, bouts of paranoia, and mental breakdowns of increasing frequency and severity. Arrested and interned for menacing a cabin steward when he returned to France in 1937 after a disastrous trip to Ireland, where he had also been arrested for threatening behavior, Artaud was subsequently lost in mental institutions during the confusion of the war. He was released from the clinic at Rodez in May of 1946, a ghostly, toothless, broken man who spent the last months of his life frantically writing and drawing to make up for nine years lost in asylums. He died of cancer on 4 March 1948.

Artaud made a final stage appearance on 13 January 1947 to read some of his recent poetry. An overcapacity crowd flocked to the Vieux Colombier Theater in Paris to hear a physically and mentally debilitated Artaud in a performance billed as "Tête-à-tête by Antonin Artaud." He gave a terrifying three-hour performance described by Gide as "atrocious, painful, almost sublime at moments, revolting also and quasi-intolerable."[5] At the end Artaud, whose glasses and manuscript had fallen to the floor, lashed out at the audience: "I put myself in your place, and I can see that what I tell you isn't at all interesting. It's still theater."[6] Later he wrote to André Breton, "One could see the so-called lecturer that wasn't I at all, in any case the supposed man of theater, renounce his spectacle, pack up and go away because I realized that there had been enough words, enough bellowing, and what was needed were bombs, but I had none in my hands, none in my pockets."[7] Twenty years earlier, Artaud had insisted at the conclusion of his "Manifesto for an Abortive Theatre" that "bombs need to be thrown . . . at the root of the majority of present-day habits of thought" (*CW2,* 25). If indeed Artaud's pockets were empty on that day in 1947, in the interval between the creation of the Alfred Jarry Theater in 1926 and the pathetic conclusion of his Vieux Colombier performance, the bombs launched by Artaud in the wake of those fired by Jarry, Dada, and surrealism had already destroyed enough of the traditional French theater to make room for the movement that was to be known as the theater of the absurd.

Part 2.
Absurdist Playwrights

Chapter Three
Samuel Beckett

Beckett's best-known metaphor for the human condition is contained in *Waiting for Godot:* an interminable lonely wait for something uncertain and probably meaningless. His plays are full of questions and inadequate replies. God is frequently evoked, but there is no heavenly response in this theater where God is afflicted with "divine apathia divine athambia divine aphasia" (*G,* 29). The human race cannot be counted on for solace either. "Oh I know," says Winnie in *Happy Days,* in a characteristically Beckettian twist of an Anglican prayer, that "it does not follow when two are gathered together—(*faltering*)—in this way—(*normal*)—that because one sees the other the other sees the one, life has taught me that . . . too."[1] Although Beckett had little faith in the possibility of human communication, his characters converse almost nonstop. "It's so we won't think. . . . It's so we won't hear. . . . All the dead voices" (*G,* 40–41). No playwright has expressed more disturbingly than Beckett both the tragic yearning for silence and endings and the comic impossibility of such silence, given the human drive to keep on talking. Beckett's appalled indictments of the irremediable difficulty of being are the richest in tragedy and comedy in of any of the plays in the theater of the absurd. "Nothing is funnier than unhappiness," Nell remarks from her trash can in *Endgame.*[2]

Background

Beckett's dramatic universe is obsessional and inwardly oriented. "The only fertile research is excavatory, immersive, a contraction of the spirit, a descent," he maintained early in his career and remained true to his dictum.[3] He writes, as A. Alvarez observes, "like someone who never had a childhood—without nostalgia, regret, vulnerability, or much discernable trace of the more undefended emotions like tenderness."[4] He was born to a prosperous Irish Protestant family in Foxrock, a suburb of Dublin, in 1906. The date on the birth certificate filed by his father is 13 May. Beckett, however, insisted that it was 13 April, enjoying the irony of a birth date that was both a Good Friday and a Friday the thirteenth.[5] He claimed to have had "a very good childhood, and a very normal childhood as childhoods go," but acknowledged being "more aware of unhappiness around me . . . than happiness."[6] From childhood on, Beckett was prone to depression and silent withdrawal.

He graduated from Trinity College, Dublin, in 1927 with top examination honors in French and Italian literature. The following year he began a two-year appointment as an exchange lecturer in English at the Ecole normale supérieure in Paris, where he was drawn into the sphere of James Joyce, a fellow Irishman who shared his love of words and of Dante. Joyce's influence is strongly reflected in the erudite punning style of Beckett's early prose. In 1929, at Joyce's request, Beckett contributed an essay entitled "Dante . . . Bruno . Vico . . Joyce" to *Our Exagmination Round His Factification for Incamination of Work in Progress,* a title given by Joyce to a series of essays by young writers that constituted a kind of prepublication exegesis of *Finnegans Wake.* Beckett's essay contains an interesting assessment of literary purgatories: "Dante's is conical and consequently implies culmination. Mr. Joyce's is spherical and excludes culmination."[7] Beckett's own purgatories, for the most part, would take the same shape as Joyce's.

During his first stay in Paris Beckett also published *Whoroscope,* a prize-winning poem on Descartes, and wrote a monograph on Proust. Much of what he has to say about Proust is predictive of his own literary concerns. "Victims" and "prisoners" are the key terms he uses to describe the relationship of Proust's characters to time. Beckett's dramatic world is also heavy with the menace of time. His characters are mired in the past and deluded by prospects for the future. "Do you believe in the life to come?" Hamm asks Clov in *Endgame.* Clov replies, as might all of Beckett's creatures, "Mine was always that" (*E,* 49). Beckett's characters, like Proust's, attempt to shield themselves from time's truths with memories and habit. But memories are notoriously faulty in Beckett's world; and habit, as he fiercely contends in *Proust* and graphically illustrates in his plays, is "the ballast that chains the dog to his vomit" (*P,* 8).

Beckett completed his M.A. at Trinity College in 1930. For most of the next three years he lived in Dublin bogged down in familial conflict, drink, and depression until an annuity from his father's estate allowed him to live independently, although not much more happily, in London. In 1934 he published a collection of short stories, *More Pricks than Kicks.* By 1936 he had completed his first novel, *Murphy,* which was rejected by 42 publishers before it was accepted for publication in 1937, the year that Beckett moved permanently to France. During the war he was active in the French Resistance, escaping from Paris in 1942 just in time to avoid being arrested by the

Gestapo. For the rest of the war he and Suzanne Dumesnil, who later became his wife, were in hiding in Roussillon, a small village in the Vaucluse. This hellish period of forced inactivity and isolation resurfaces in the anguished interminable wait in *Godot.*

When Beckett was finally able to settle again in Paris in 1946, he entered an extraordinarily productive period. Between 1946 and 1950, writing in French, he completed another novel, *Mercier et Camier,* and worked on some of the short prose works published later as *Nouvelles et textes pour rien* (*Stories and Texts for Nothing*). He also wrote his trilogy of novels—*Molloy, Malone Dies,* and *The Unnamable*—and two plays—*Eleutheria,* which has never been staged, and *Godot,* written as "a relief from the terrible kind of prose I was writing at that time."[8] With *Godot* his reputation as a writer was finally established. Although *Godot* brought Beckett almost instant fame when it finally opened in Paris in 1953, it had taken Roger Blin, the director who had the vision and tenacity to see it through to its first production, nearly three years to find a theater for it.

The worldwide success of *Godot* did not alter Beckett's fundamental shyness or make him any less a literary recluse. He maintained a stubbornly private existence devoted primarily to dramatic writing, translating his own works, and, later in his career, directing his own plays. He remained wary of literary critics and interviews and even in his clarifications for the actors and directors who staged his plays tended to skirt symbolic interpretations. "I feel that the only line is to refuse to be involved in exegesis of any kind," he wrote to the director of an American production of *Endgame.* "My work," he added, "is a matter of fundamental sounds (no joke intended) made as fully as possible, and I accept responsibility for nothing else. If people want to have headaches among the overtones, let them. And provide their own aspirin."[9] When Beckett was awarded the Nobel Prize in literature in 1969, still avoiding the public eye, he did not go to Stockholm to collect it. He died in Paris on 22 December 1989 at age 83.

En attendant Godot (Waiting for Godot)

In 1927, during his last year at Trinity College, Beckett had frequented vaudeville performances and had been drawn to the movies of Charlie Chaplin and Laurel and Hardy. *Waiting for Godot,* written two decades later, merges the slapstick comedy and pratfalls of those popular entertainments with Beckett's own painful experience of waiting for both personal and political liberation in Vichy France. Perhaps its best summary is Vladimir's line: "Hope deferred maketh the something sick" (*G,* 8). The slapstick framework transforms Beckett's personal material into a generalized portrait of the human condition that is as richly and comically physical as it is darkly poetic and metaphysical. Beckett labeled *Godot* a "tragicomedy in two acts" when he translated it into English.[10] Jean Anouilh described it as "a music-hall sketch of Pascal's *Pensées* as played by the Fratellini clowns."[11]

The first of the play's two acts begins with a remarkably spare description of the stage: "A country road. A tree. Evening." On this nearly bare set two old derelicts, who are listed as Vladimir and Estragon but who call themselves only by the childish nicknames Didi and Gogo, wait, for reasons that have become unclear, for someone named Godot. They have been together for a long time, "blathering about nothing in particular for half a century," and have shared better days: "Hand in hand from the top of the Eiffel Tower, among the first. We were respectable in those days. Now it's too late. They wouldn't even let us up" (*G,* 7). No explanation is given for their present circumstances. Beckett's characters, as he said of Proust's, "are presented and developed with a fine Dostoevskian contempt for the vulgarity of plausible concatenation" (*P,* 62). Vladimir and Estragon look like hybrids of Charlie Chaplin's tramp figure and circus clowns. They are shabbily dressed, but sport bowler hats that serve in their vaudeville routines.[12] Both walk stiffly, Vladimir because he suffers from prostate trouble and must make frequent trips offstage for relief, Estragon because his feet hurt. Estragon's ill-fitting boots start the play on a prophetically negative note. Defeated by the struggle to pull on his boot that occupies the opening moments of *Godot,* Estragon gives up, saying: "Nothing to be done." His words are snatched up but their meaning comically misconstrued by the more philosophical Vladimir, who responds: "I'm beginning to come round to that opinion. All my life I've tried to put it from me, saying, Vladimir, be reasonable, you haven't yet tried everything" (*G,* 7). The minds and memories of the more readily prone and infantile Estragon and the upright, motherly Vladimir intersect, like the tree and the road, without marking any useful bearings.

Vladimir and Estragon spend their time trying not to acknowledge that "there's no lack of the void." What they find to do "to give us the impression we exist" was both shockingly trivial and indecorous for the theater of the early 1950s. They fiddle with their hats and boots. Estragon eats the blackened radishes and turnips that Vladimir retrieves from the rubbish in his large Harpo Marx–like pockets. They sleep, spit, urinate, do their exercises, and fart. Vladimir has trouble with his unbuttoned fly; Estragon loses his pants at the end of the play. Early in the first act they consider hanging themselves for the pleasure of the erection that reportedly accompanies the event but abandon the project for fear that the bough might break with its first victim, leaving one of them out. The physical world is as inimical to their needs as the spiritual. They are plagued with infirmities, and the slapstick props are useless or treacherous. Shoes cause pain, pants won't cooperate, dirty "carrots" turn out to be turnips, trees and rope belts won't even do for a hanging, and the comically itchy hats set thought in motion, an activity best avoided. Above all the two tramps pass the time batting words back and forth. Existence has become a verbal ball game in which the ball is all too often dropped by an uncooperative player. They argue childishly, insult each other, tell stories, recite poetry, sing, reminisce as much as Estragon's recalcitrant and cranky memory permits, consider repenting the sin of being born, and occasionally support each other with lyrical interchanges that turn the play momentarily into an exquisite poem. The only speech act that is not permitted is the recital of a nightmare.

Godot does not arrive. Three other characters do: a master-and-slave couple and a messenger boy. Just after Estragon asks nervously if he and Vladimir are tied to Godot, Lucky, a literal wreck of a human being burdened with a heavy bag, a folding stool, a picnic basket, and an overcoat, reaches center stage at the end of a long rope. The crack of a whip announces his master, Pozzo, exaggeratedly decked out as a prosperous landowner, who make his appearance at the other end of the rope. Estragon mistakes Pozzo for Godot.[13] Pozzo and Lucky also wear bowler hats. These hats are necessary to the process of thinking in this vaudeville act that passes for existence. They are also a comical means of tying the four characters together as representatives of Everyman, an insistent theme of the play. "You are human beings nonetheless," Pozzo observes of Vladimir and Estragon, adding, as he bursts into an enormous laugh: "Of the same species as Pozzo! Made in God's image" (*G,* 15). At the end of the second act, Estragon, who has addressed the collapsed Pozzo as both Cain and Abel and elicited a cry for help with both names, observes indifferently to Vladimir: "He's all humanity" (*G,* 54). Beckett blows up the Everyman theme to comic proportions by choosing names for the four characters that suggest a broad geographical base and the animal, vegetable, and mineral kingdoms: Vladimir is a Russian name; Pozzo is Italian for "well" or "hole"; Estragon is a French herb (tarragon); and the English name Lucky is a more likely choice for a horse or a dog than a man.

Beckett's first plays are all populated by ham actors. In *Godot* Pozzo entertains with the ostentatious tossing of a chicken bone from his otherwise unshared picnic and a lyrically self-satisfied soliloquy on the night sky, which he deflates at the end with a very Beckettian observation: "That's how it is on this bitch of an earth" (*G,* 25). Lucky, on command from Pozzo, dances and thinks out loud. The placing of Lucky's hat on his head sets off an alarming monologue whose philosophical underpinnings have been minutely analyzed but whose effect in performance is akin to Dadaist dementia. In 1974, when he was directing *Godot* in Berlin, Beckett told the actors that Lucky's speech could be divided into three parts. The first part, according to Beckett, is about "the indifference of heaven, about divine apathy"; the second is "about man who is shrinking—about man, who is dwindling"; and the third is about "the earth abode of stones."[14] For the unsuspecting observer, however, who is subjected to a rapidly delivered discourse that begins, "Given the existence as uttered forth in the public works of Puncher and Wattmann of a personal God quaquaquaqua with white beard quaquaquaqua outside time without extension who from the heights of divine apathia divine athambia divine aphasia loves us dearly with some exceptions for reasons unknown but time will tell" (*G,* 28), little is fathomable beyond the initial notion of an apathetic God whose ways are as mysteriously erratic as those of the absent Godot. A few other words and phrases stick by repetition. The phrase "for reasons unknown" punctuates the text ten times, "but time will tell" four times, and "unfinished" seven times. "Unfinished" is the last word spoken before Lucky is silenced. There are references to sports of all kinds, real and imaginary. The game of tennis in particular crops up eight times and the word "skull" is repeated eight times in the last thirteen lines of text. Thus, from all the babble, what emerges with the impact of a physical blow is the basic proposition in Beckett's writing that life is some kind of a skull game that "for reasons unknown" cannot end. The initial laughter provoked by what appears at first to be simply a hilarious parody of academic discourse fizzles into pained amazement as the avalanche of disconnected phrases and misplaced philosophical jargon is delivered with an inhumanly mechanical rapidity. There is relief on both sides of the footlights when Vladimir puts a stop to the linguistic anarchy by removing Lucky's hat. Pozzo departs with Lucky, intending to sell him at a fair. A little boy comes to announce that Godot won't be coming that night but the next. At the end of the act Estragon asks, "Well, shall we go?" Vladimir replies, "Yes, let's go" (*G,* 36). Neither Vladimir nor Estragon moves.

In act 2 the pattern of activity seems so alarmingly like that of act 1 that it prompted Vivian Mercier's remark that *Godot* is a play where "nothing happens twice."[15] The stage directions read: "Next day. Same time. Same place." Estragon's ill-fitting boots are carefully placed center front in the splayed position of Charlie Chaplin's feet. Estragon has once more spent the night in a ditch and been beaten. They again consider suicide but put it off until the next day because the cord that holds up Estragon's pants is inadequate as a hanging rope. Vladimir and Estragon keep on talking and waiting. Godot does not arrive, only Pozzo and Lucky once again and the little boy with the news that Godot will not be coming that evening but the next.

The second act is shorter and crueler and there are some changes, but the changes do not point to any meaningful conclusion. The four or five leaves sprouted by the tree that was barren in the first act are a mockery, not an affirmation of cyclical rebirth. The conversational ball gets dropped more often into painful silences. The pratfalls become more appallingly symbolic and the comical irony of the Everyman theme grows blacker. When Pozzo and Lucky return, Pozzo is blind and Lucky is mute. Lucky falls down immediately upon arrival, as he did in act 1, but in act 2 he takes Pozzo down with him. Listening to the fallen Pozzo's cries for help, Vladimir observes that these cries are addressed to all mankind and remarks that "at this moment of time, all mankind is us whether we like it or not" (*G,* 51). "All mankind" does not lift up the fallen pair, however, because it is too busy talking and trying to figure out what compensation might be extracted for the service. When Vladimir does finally extend his hand to Pozzo, he falls too. Eventually, in a parody of the biblical fall, all four characters lie in a tangled heap. Pozzo, callously lyric in the first act, becomes broodingly philosophical in the second. Exploding in impatience at Vladimir's questions about when Pozzo became blind and Lucky mute, he lashes out: "When! When! One day, is that not enough for you, one day he went dumb, one day I went blind, one day we'll go deaf, one day we were born, one day we shall die, the same day, the same second, is that not enough for you? . . . They give birth astride of a grave, the light gleams an instant, then it's night once more" (*G,* 57). A preoccupation with death is one of the central themes in the theater of the absurd, but Beckett's approach to it is unique. In his plays it is not the inevitability of death that makes it so terrible, but the fact that even though "the whole universe stinks of corpses," death doesn't quite finish its job. Vladimir picks up the thread of Pozzo's speech and embroiders it: "Astride of a grave and a difficult birth. Down in the hole, lingeringly, the grave-digger puts on the forceps. We have time to grow old. The air is full of our cries. . . . But habit is a great deadener" (*G,* 58–59). At the end of act 2 it is Vladimir who says, "Yes, let's go." Again, neither Vladimir nor Estragon moves.

Although the curtain does not rise again for a third act or a fourth or a fifth, following the same pattern and ending with the same words, Beckett has made it clear that it could. The traditional concept of dramatic tension does not apply to a performance of *Godot,* where the uneasy audience waits uncomfortably with Vladimir and Estragon for these futile discussions and pratfalls to end. There is, however, an even more fundamental tension generated by the delicate balance necessary to keep the circular structure intact. The circle is tenuously cemented by the paralyzing contradictory fears that move Vladimir's and Estragon's minds and mouths but trap them physically on this desolate stretch of road. The apprehension that this unbearable repetitive nothingness will go on and on is countered by the dread of an event or arrival that could cause the ball of habit to be irretrievably dropped. The tramps' instinctive response in the first act to the terrible cry that precedes the arrival of Pozzo and Lucky is to run "cringing away from the menace."

Volumes of criticism have been devoted to *Godot*. It is a play in which every element, from the tree to the vegetables to the ropes to the absent presence of the title character lends itself to multiple interpretations: "In a text so spare, so cunningly random, everything is a lure. . . . all images, the more off-handed the more suspicious, loom as potential motifs in the grand design."[16] The most extensive debate about Beckett's "grand design" has been on the subject of who or what is Godot? Martin Esslin, who began his landmark study of the theater of the absurd with a description of a 1957 performance of the play at the San Quentin penitentiary, quotes a reporter who claimed that the prisoners had no difficulty understanding the play. According to one prisoner Godot was "society," for another he was "the outside" (Esslin, 20). For most audiences, however, just as for Vladimir and Estragon, the identity of Godot has been more mysterious. Interpretations have run the gamut from "happiness, eternal life, the unattainable quest of all men" to "a bicycle racer, Time Future, and a Paris street for call girls."[17] Because biblical references and religious symbols come up so often, a persistent critical approach has been to treat Godot as a diminutive of God equivalent to the diminutive "Charlot," as Charlie Chaplin was affectionately known in France. The groundwork for a religious interpretation is laid almost immediately in the play when Vladimir, in one of his first attempts to keep the conversation going, delves into the enigma of the Gospels' contradictory accounts of the two thieves crucified with Christ, one of whom was supposedly saved, the other not. Although Estragon characteristically dismisses the problem with the observation that "People are bloody ignorant apes" (*G,* 9), the arbitrary nature of divine justice, which tortures Vladimir, does seem to be related to the unpredictable Godot, who, according to the shepherd-boy messenger, is good to him but beats his brother, the goatherd. Beckett, however, has stoutly maintained that if he had meant God he would have said so, explaining thus his abundant use of Christian symbolism in his plays: "Christianity is a mythology with which I am perfectly familiar. So naturally I use it" (Duckworth, 18). Frederick Busi argues reasonably that "Beckett is not really interested in refuting, even less so in affirming Christian values. He is taken by Christianity's intellectual history, by the patterns and shapes it has assumed" (Busi, 77). Only one thing is certain: Godot is a fixture in an agonized wait by creatures who are chained by the "ballast of habit." For Beckett, the fact and the nature of the wait and the men who are waiting were more important than any particular definition of Godot. The pain of the wait is tempered only by the difficult friendship that binds Vladimir and Estragon. However, since Beckett once described friendship as "a social expedient, like upholstery or the distribution of garbage buckets," even that may be merely a reflection of the need that is constantly voiced in his plays to be seen by someone and to have an ear available for conversation (*P,* 46).

Godot, which has become the best-known and best-loved play in the absurdist repertory, won acceptance quickly. Vladimir and Estragon, dumped in an existential puzzle where too many pieces are missing or malformed, exist as flesh-and-blood creatures in a way that theater of the absurd characters almost never do. Ruby Cohn's reaction to one of the early performances of *Godot* in France captures its very human appeal: "I had never heard of Beckett when I first saw *Godot.* I did not know my Bible well enough to recognize the scriptural kernel of the play. I had not read Hegel's *Phenomenology of Mind* well enough to recognize the archetypical Master-slave relationship. I was not even a devotee of silent comic films. . . . And yet I knew almost at once that those two French-speaking tramps were me; more miserable, more lovable, more humorous, more desperate" (Cohn, 127–28). *Godot* has been made into an opera, a movie, and scenarios for dance. Unauthorized sequels have been written, and even Brecht wanted to write his own version of it. As Alan Schneider once remarked, *Godot* is "no longer a play but a condition of life."[18]

Fin de partie (Endgame)

Endgame, written in French in 1955 and 1956, is also about waiting and numbing the pain of existence with words. "What is there to keep me here?" Clov asks. "The dialogue," Hamm replies (*E,* 58). The title refers to the final moments of a chess game, when the king's position is threatened. In this stalemated match the hostile verbal interchanges, measured physical movements, and threatening silences are all attempts to hold one's own position and weaken the other's defenses. *Endgame,* like *Godot,* introduces two pairs of aged, infirm characters gallingly at odds but bound by the need for an audience and by dependencies created by physical afflictions: Hamm, the master; Clov, his servant; and Hamm's parents, Nagg and Nell, who are confined to garbage cans, expiating the result of their "accursed" fornication. Nagg and Nell have lost their legs long ago in a tandem bicycle accident. Hamm can't stand. Clov can't sit. Hamm is blind and paralyzed. Clov can still get around and can still see, but his legs are bad and his eyes are going. With cruel relish Hamm predicts Clov's future: "One day you'll be blind, like me. You'll be sitting there, a speck in the void, in the dark, for ever, like me. . . . Infinite emptiness will be all around you, all the resurrected dead of all the ages wouldn't fill it, and there you'll be like a little bit of grit in the middle of the steppe" (*E,* 36). The names are punningly evocative of all sorts of roles and relationships, from kitchen ingredients to a tragic Shakespearean figure and biblical catastrophes.[19] Appropriately, in this play in which Hamm nails his human appendages into his fictions, Clov's name is very close to *clou,* the French word for nail, and Nagg's to *nagel,* German for nail. Nell is related to nail both by sound and the fact that she is also called Pegg. The hammer-nail connection would also seem to suggest the hammering of a lid onto a coffin in a play where the theme of death is omnipresent. However, as Clov informs Hamm, there are no more coffins. The final darkness is not accessible. Although Nell finally falls silent and is therefore presumed dead, the other characters appear to have been sentenced to decay into eternity.

Endgame is played on a nearly bare, gray-lit stage in a space Hamm refers to as the "old shelter." It begins with a brief still life. Clov stands motionless by the door. Hamm, center stage in his chair on casters, is covered by a sheet. The garbage cans that house Nagg and Nell are also covered. Clov breaks up the tableau with a long, precise pantomime suggestive of chess moves. He stands first under each of the two windows high up at the back of the stage. Then he fetches a ladder, mounts it, draws back the curtains at each window, descends, and mounts the ladder again to look out each window, uttering a brief laugh each time he looks out. Finally, he removes the sheet covering two ash bins, peers in each, laughs, and uncovers Hamm, who has a large blood-stained handkerchief over his face and a whistle around his neck for summoning Clov. After another brief laugh, Clov turns toward the audience and tonelessly announces the endgame: "Finished, it's finished, nearly finished, it must be nearly finished." At last, a bored

Hamm removes his bloody "old stancher" and makes the first move: "Me— / (he yawns) / —to play" (*E,* 2). Much of Hamm's "play" is in the form of a sadistic autobiographical chronicle, which he invents and recites with Pozzo-like histrionics and critiques. Hamm is a ham actor who keeps himself going by providing his own stage directions. He tells of a man who came to him one Christmas Eve begging for bread for his very small son. Hamm, playing Hamm and relishing his power and cruelty, berates the man for bringing another creature into the world, but offers to take the man and the child into his service. It is possible that the little boy is Clov.

Endgame, described by one of its directors as "the crisis of exhaustion playing itself out in the suburbs of hell," is a bleaker version than *Godot* of human existence as a pointless loitering in time.[20] There are no possibly redeeming flashes of affection. When Beckett directed the play in Germany he told the actors playing Hamm and Clov: "From the first exchange between the two, maximum hostility must be played. Your war is the nucleus of the play.[21] Clov plays cruel tricks on Hamm even as he does his capricious bidding, and Hamm behaves viciously toward Clov. The comedy of their witty repartee arises from a sadistic humor, which they both indulge freely in their treatment of Nagg and Nell. Outside the strange shelter there is no life, no scenery, no sound, only dead gray light. There is no hope for salvation. The mere thought that "something is taking its course" or that some other form of life might be left to keep "this" going is intolerable. Clov becomes nearly hysterical in his effort to destroy a flea, one of the few circus-like moments in this very dark play. Hamm and Clov are desperate to eradicate a mouse, and they treat Clov's possible sighting of a young boy in the distance as an unspeakable disaster. The barren isolation of the "old shelter" where Clov's seeds won't sprout and everything is running out—not only coffins, but bicycle wheels, pap, and bonbons for Nagg—has led to speculation that *Endgame* takes place in the aftermath of a nuclear explosion. Hugh Kenner's likening of the stage with its high windows to the interior of an immense skull, however, is a much more Beckettian approach.[22] Kenner's comparison captures the horror of an existence that can't be made to end because the fabricating mind, which is Beckett's peculiar version of the avenging mythological Furies, won't let go.

The final moments of *Endgame* are characteristically ambiguous. What seems to be the end may simply be the setting of the stage for another performance by Hamm. Clov, dressed in outlandish traveling clothes, has set an alarm clock to signal that he has abandoned Hamm and not simply died in his kitchen. Nell's and Nagg's trash cans are again covered with their sheets. Thinking that the silent Clov has left, Hamm intones one more time, "Me to play," and delivers with all the usual dramatic flourishes a last soliloquy: "Old endgame lost of old, play and lose and have done losing. . . . Moments for nothing, now as always, time was never and time is over, reckoning closed and story ended" (*E,* 82–83). He replaces his bloody "old stancher" just as it was when the play began. Clov does not leave. Silently halted by the door with his eyes fixed on Hamm, he too resumes his initial posture in the play. In chess, mobility is essential to victory. Clov is as stuck as Hamm. Even if the stalemate could be broken, the game would be for naught. When a mistake is made in the setting up of the chess board, the game must be declared void. In Beckett's world the mere fact of coming into existence is to be "set" wrong. *Endgame* was Beckett's favorite of his plays.

Of *Endgame,* whose blackness has continued to challenge directors, actors, and audiences, Beckett wrote: "Rather difficult and elliptic, mostly depending on the power of the text to claw, more inhuman than 'Godot.'"[23] Roger Blin, who directed the first *Endgame* and played Hamm, had to take the production to the Royal Court Theatre in London in April 1957 for its world premiere in French because he was unable to find a Paris theater willing to take the risk. In general, it was badly received in London. *Godot* had not prepared audiences for a spectacle as relentlessly depressing as *Endgame.* Kenneth Tynan reported that "last week's production, portentously stylized, piled on the agony until I thought my skull would split."[24] When Blin brought it back to Paris later that month, it fared somewhat better and lasted through 97 performances.

Krapp's Last Tape

In *Krapp's Last Tape,* written in English in 1958, Beckett introduces a solitary player, the brooding, unshaven old Krapp. White-faced, purple-nosed, dressed in grimy ill-fitting clothes and enormous boots, tippling, eating bananas, and slipping on the peel, Krapp is a derelict clown whose performance graphically illustrates Beckett's contention that "the attempt to communicate where no communication is possible is merely a simian vulgarity, or horribly comic" (*P,* 46). Krapp is alone on stage, but he does not deliver a monologue. As much in need of another voice and ear as any other of Beckett's characters, he carries on a conversation with his own taped voice. The occasion for his "last tape" is a ritual recording on his sixty-ninth birthday of the elapsed year's highlights. Because there was little of note beyond "the sour cud and the iron stool,"[25] Krapp spends most of his time listening to a tape made on his thirty-ninth birthday.

Beckett makes brilliant use of a reel of tape and a ledger in which Krapp has recorded the tape's themes—"Mother at rest at last. . . . The black ball. . . . Slight improvement in bowel condition. . . . Equinox, memorable equinox. . . . Farewell to . . . love" (*SP,* 57)—to explore the themes of memory and habit, those attributes of the "Time cancer," as he called them in *Proust*. *Krapp's Last Tape* replays the premise of *Godot* and *Endgame:* not only is life hopelessly repetitious, but each repetition is increasingly vitiated by time and habit. Krapp is separated from his taped past by poor hearing, shortsightedness, and failing memory. He has trouble reading the ledger and has to look up one of his old words in a dictionary. His affective impoverishment is reflected in the coarse scorn elicited by the 39-year-old Krapp's taped response to a memory of an afternoon in his late twenties spent in a gently rocking boat with his face on a woman's breasts. The still ambitious middle-aged Krapp dismisses the scene with a rationalization: "Perhaps my best years are gone. When there was a chance of happiness. But I wouldn't want them back. Not with the fire in me now. No, I wouldn't want them back" (*SP,* 63). Old Krapp sneers at the lyrical outbursts of "that stupid bastard I took myself for thirty years ago" and adds, "Thank God that's all done with anyway" (*SP,* 62). He replays the scene three times, however, and has just listened to it again when the play ends with a mute, motionless Krapp staring straight ahead into nothingness while the tape runs on into silence.

Unlike *Godot* and *Endgame, Krapp's Last Tape* focuses on an imminent end. Twice Krapp sings the hymn "Now the Days Are Over." In the earlier plays this kind of repetition would have signalled that the days were simply eternally ending, but Krapp's situation is different. He is running out of words, a sure sign of death in Beckett's theater. Krapp's frequent references to his constipation are more than obvious puns on his name. The affliction matches the verbal constriction that is closing down his existence. According to Jean Martin, who was Beckett's first Lucky and first Clov and played Krapp in a 1977 production: "Sam has always said that on the morning after the play Krapp was surely *dead*. He has always insisted on the fact that Krapp is debris. Some sort of an old man with hardly any age at all and just before his end" (McMillan and Fehsenfeld, 257).

Krapp points the way to Beckett's later short plays, where physical effects, particularly mime and stage lighting, take over almost entirely as "text." His odd dialogue involves an elaborate physical routine, beginning, as *Endgame* did, with a pantomime highlighting the minimal props that constitute a shriveling universe. He fumbles nearsightedly with an old envelope and his keys and interacts with a mindless sensuality with his first banana, which he strokes, peels, and sticks in his mouth for a while as he stares blankly before him. He mimes a masturbatory relationship to his tape recorder and responds with elaborate facial and body gestures as he visualizes the words on the tape that capture his attention.[26] Krapp's mental arena is delimited by a strong white light that circumscribes his chair and table and the tape recorder. The rest of the stage, a projection of the physical world that he has rejected, is left in darkness. The stage light mirrors the symbolic play of light in Krapp's taped words. In the segment made on Krapp's thirty-ninth birthday that describes his mother's death, the balance of light and dark suggested by the allusion to the "memorable equinox" is tipped toward death and darkness. The images of whiteness are overshadowed by dark images: the "deep weeds of viduity"; the black plumage of a bird; a "dark young beauty . . . all white and starch" pushing a black-hooded baby carriage, "most funereal thing"; a white dog playing with a black ball. The dimming creates a deadening effect similar to Beckett's description of Proustian voluntary memory, which "presents the past in monochrome" (*P,* 19). Krapp's past has become a dark and useless fiction.

Beckett, who had been closely involved with the final rehearsals for the premiere performance of *Krapp's Last Tape* in London in 1958 on a double bill with *Endgame,* was bitterly disappointed by the critics' cool reception. Kenneth Tynan dismissed them both in a parody entitled *Slamm's Last Knock.* The New York and Paris productions in 1960, the latter in Beckett's own translation, were more successful. Robert Brustein described *Krapp* as "the perfect realization of Beckett's idea of human isolation."[27]

Happy Days

The ironically titled *Happy Days,* written in English in 1960–61, opens with an arresting surrealistic image: In a mound, centered under a relentless light on a stage representing an expanse of scorched grass, the heroine is buried up to her waist. Winnie, "about fifty, well preserved, blond for preference, plump, arms and shoulders bare, low bodice, big bosom, pearl necklet," is flanked on either side by a large black shopping bag and a closed parasol. Behind her but hidden by the mound is her husband, Willie. Winnie is asleep. Awakened by a strident bell, she looks up at the blazing sun, comments that it is "another heavenly day," and concludes aloud the prayer she has been mouthing, "World without end Amen" (*HD,* 8). No reason is given for Winnie's burial. She recalls a man passing by who wondered, as the spectator does: "What's she doing . . . What's the idea . . . stuck up to her diddies in the bleeding ground . . . What does it mean . . .

What's it meant to mean . . . ?" His wife's retort is the kind of answer one gets to such questions from Beckett: "And you . . . what's the idea of you . . . what are you meant to mean?" (*HD,* 42–43). Winnie does what Beckett's male protagonists have done before her: She performs banal ceremonies with the few props left her—the toothbrush, lipstick, nail file, spectacles, and hat that she pulls from her black bag—and uses her mouth to create an existence. She is strangely indifferent to running out of her medicine, an antidote to "loss of spirits . . . lack of keenness . . . want of appetite," and, although she trifles affectionately with a revolver that she takes from her purse, she does not consider using it.

Winnie is another of Beckett's inveterate performers, providing her own stage directions for encouragement, miming her own words, and altering her voice to play all the necessary roles in her narrative stratagems. Her verbal facade is pockmarked by silences that are sometimes theatrical and sometimes threatening, and she falters on occasion: "Words fail, there are times when even they fail" (*HD,* 24). Nevertheless, like her predecessors, she needs just to know that somewhere there is another ear or voice, however indifferent or hostile, in order to go on talking, praying, singing, telling stories, and quoting and misquoting playwrights and poets. Even the very few words uttered by the obstinately silent Willie suffice: "Just to know that in theory you can hear me even though in fact you don't is all I need" (*HD,* 27). Winnie's repeated "No better, no worse, no change, no pain" is an appalling acknowledgment of the deadening function of habit. The irony of her opening words and the ritual "world without end" closing to her prayer contain the essence of Beckett's world: words that become word-worlds without end.

Beckett returns in this play to a two-act format to create a *Godot*-like effect of grinding on in repetitive circles. In act 2, Winnie is buried up to her neck in the mound. Her immobilized head rigidly faces front during the entire act. The black bag and the conspicuous revolver lie uselessly beside her. Her parasol, which explodes in a surrealistic spontaneous combustion in the first act, is back in place in the second, just as she had predicted. The much shorter second act mirrors the shrinking of Winnie's resources but also suggests that the existence that spins from her ever-resourceful mind would go on even if she were to disappear completely into the mound. Musing about "The Earthball," Winnie reflects that "there always remains something" and sums up her sentence to a purgatory in the skull: "If the mind were to go. (*Pause.*) It won't of course. (*Pause.*) Not quite" (*HD,* 52). Significantly, the bell that supposedly ends Winnie's day is never actually heard, and the blazing sun never sets. Even with her physical range reduced to facial expressions and voice changes, the actress playing Winnie must convey nearly the same degree of frenetic carrying on in the second act as in the first.

At the end of act 2 Willie makes a surprising move. On all fours and "dressed to kill" in a top hat, morning coat, and striped trousers, he crawls round Winnie's mound and struggles unsuccessfully to climb it. No hint reveals whether Willie wants Winnie, as she supposes, or the gun that lies uselessly next to her. Defeated and flat on the ground, Willie says his only word in the second act, an ironic abbreviation of his wife's name to "Win." The unexpected diversion is initially given a chilly reception by Winnie. Willie's appearance threatens to create what Beckett described as "the perilous zones in the life of the individual, dangerous, precarious, painful, mysterious and fertile, when for a moment the boredom of living is replaced by the suffering of being" (*P*, 8). When the safely prone Willie utters his word, however, Winnie pronounces it a "happy day" and begins to sing a music box dance tune.

Happy Days had its premiere in New York in 1961, where it ran for 100 performances. It opened in Paris in 1963 in a translation by Beckett, directed by Roger Blin and with Madeleine Renaud, one of France's most extraordinary actresses, playing Winnie. Critics were wildly enthusiastic. Even the critic for *Le Monde,* previously unflattering to Beckett, described the production as "one of the theater marvels of all times" and suggested, "Perhaps one would have to go back to Aeschylus's *Prometheus* to find such a pure dramatization of solitude."[28]

Dramaticules

The radio plays Beckett wrote immediately after *Happy Days*—*Words and Music, Rough for Radio I, Cascando,* and *Rough for Radio II*—announce his future "dramaticules." In *Words and Music,* two of the three characters, Words and Music, are abstractions, although the third character, Croak, refers to them as Bob and Joe. They speak in disjointed poetic fragments of old age and love that could not be won. The last sound is a profound sigh. Beckett's later plays are short, physical, and starkly abstract. He continues to treat the same basic themes and to structure his theater in claustrophobically repetitious circles, but these short plays emphasize visual imagery, mime, and rhythmic play of sound and light over the spoken text. The words become more and more difficult for the spectator to follow. "Action" is increasingly restricted to fragmented, repetitive patterns of light and movement. The abstracted characters, for the most part old minds churning ancient grudges and disasters, are as confined and disembodied as Winnie and belong much more often than in the earlier plays to women. No longer in pairs, the characters are frequently part of a trio or appear on stage alone.

Play, written in English in 1963, consists of only 11 pages of text, followed by three pages of notes on its intricate stage patterns. It is a transition from the "sweet old style," as Winnie keeps saying in her unwitting parody of Dante, to the very brief stage plays. The equivocal title is a complex punning allusion to the work itself as a piece of dramatic fiction, to the sexual play that preoccupies its discarnate characters, to the kind of existential play-acting that keeps all of Beckett's characters going, to the play of light that provokes speech, and to the musical effect of its repetitive patterns and rhythms. The curtain rises on a darkened stage where from three contiguous, identical gray urns protrude the impassive faces of two women, W1 and W2, and a man, M, "so lost to age and aspect as to seem almost part of the urns" (*SP,* 147). Like Winnie's in the second act of *Happy Days,* their heads are fixed face forward. Only the faces are lit by a swivelling spotlight. The light, according to Beckett's notes, functions like a "unique inquisitor" (*SP,* 158). It stimulates the players to intone their misery and controls their speech patterns.

Play is a fragmented *monologue à trois* about a ménage à trois in which W1, W2, and M were all once involved. Their earthy ruminations, chewed cudlike for years, are to be played like the antics in *Godot* for a bawdy comic effect. At the same time, the fragmented rhythmic delivery of the lines must convey the painful, incomprehensible banging of the word-churning mind against the drive to let go. As in *Godot, Endgame,* and *Happy Days,* any attempt to generate momentum threatens the protective barrier of habit. "On the other hand," W2 worries, "things may disimprove, there is that danger" (*SP,* 153). The darkness that threatens beyond the spotlight is both irresistible and terrifying.

After *Play,* Beckett's theater shrinks to "dramaticules," a term he coined in 1965 for his *Come and Go,* which even with elaborate notes takes up only three pages of printed text. Beckett's condensed dramatic productions from the late 1960s to the mid-1980s might be labeled "minimalist theater of the absurd." Many of them were written for specific actors or occasions. With the exception of *Catastrophe* and *What Where,* they were written in English. *Come and Go* is also a "play" of light and speech against darkness and silence; the characters speak only in the light. A spotlight is projected on three nearly identical women of indeterminate age, disembodied by long coats wrapping them neck to foot. They have the ironically down-to-earth names of Vi, Ru, and Flo, but their first line—"When did we three last meet?" (*SP,* 194)—turns them into burlesque versions of the witches in

Macbeth. With the rest of the stage in darkness and the bench where they are lined up at the beginning of the play so dimly lit as to be barely visible, they appear to be suspended in space. The action consists of a configuration of silent, invisible exits and entrances, which generate fragments of reminiscences and foreboding gossip about the temporarily absent member of the trio. At the end, the three women weave a chain of their arms in order to "hold hands in the old way." Flo says "I can feel the rings," but there are no rings visible on their well-lit hands (*SP,* 195). The curtain falls on this tableau of lives that have come, twisted together, and gone, but have not ended.

Breath, written in the mid-1960s for Kenneth Tynan's erotic revue *Oh! Calcutta!* (from which it was later withdrawn because Tynan took liberties with the staging), is a 30- second "performance" on a rubbish-strewn stage without actors and without words. It consists of an amplified recording of the inhalation and exhalation of a breath, accompanied by a minutely regulated increase and decrease of the stage light and punctuated by two identical brief cries: "instant of recorded vagitus," according to Beckett's notation (*SP,* 211). Beckett gave a characteristically tongue-in-cheek description of it as "a farce in five acts" (Fletcher and Fletcher, 207). *Not I* (1972) reduces the human presence to a talking mouth. Unlike Tzara's *The Gas Heart,* in which Mouth was represented by a full person, in *Not I* Mouth is only that: the mouth of a real actress whose face and body are otherwise invisible in the dark. While a silent, hooded auditor of indeterminate sex stands silently down stage, raising and dropping his arms as he listens "in a gesture of helpless compassion," Mouth, flanked by a black bag like Winnie's, delivers a very brief monologue embroidering on essential Beckettian motifs: "All the time something begging . . . something in her begging . . . begging it all to stop . . . unanswered . . . prayer unanswered . . . or unheard . . . too faint . . . so on . . . keep on . . . trying . . . not knowing what" (*SP,* 222).

That Time and *Footfalls* were first performed in London in 1976 as part of a triple bill with *Play. That Time* is a condensation of *Krapp.* An old, white-faced auditor, whose dimly lit face on an otherwise dark stage appears to be suspended about ten feet above the floor, listens, breathing audibly, to projections of his own voice relaying memories. The brief prefatory note is a good example of the technical complexity of these short plays: "Moments of one and the same voice A B C relay one another without solution of continuity—apart from the two 10-second breaks. Yet the switch from one to another must be clearly faintly perceptible" (*SP,* 227). The words of the last voice to speak in *That Time* may be Beckett's "exegesis" of *Breath:* "not a sound only the old breath and the leaves turning and then suddenly this dust whole place suddenly full of dust when you opened your eyes from floor to ceiling nothing only dust and not a sound only what was it it said come and gone was that it something like that come and gone come and gone no one come and gone in no time gone in no time" (*SP,* 235). In *Footfalls,* M, a dishevelled gray-haired woman named May, which is what Beckett's family called his mother, paces back and forth across the stage conversing with the disembodied voice of her 90-year-old mother, which issues from the darkness upstage. M's long final monologue, spoken as she fades away into darkness, echoes the haunting questions, empty silences, and vague answers that thread through all of Becketts's theater: "Will you never have done? (*Pause.*) Will you never have done . . . revolving it all? (*Pause.*) It? (*Pause.*) It all. (*Pause.*) In your poor mind. (*Pause.*) It all. (*Pause.*) It all" (*SP,* 243).

Beckett's next three plays were all written in response to requests. David Warrilow, an actor who had performed roles in many of Beckett's plays, asked for the play that became *A Piece of Monologue* in 1979. The monologue is delivered by a white-haired speaker, dressed in a white nightgown and white socks and standing next to a faintly lit "skull-sized globe lamp," who ruminates on a loveless existence while "waiting on the rip word" (*SP,* 269). As is true for most of Beckett's characters, the likelihood of the Speaker resting in peace is slim. Although his lamp goes out at the end of the play, the repetitive nature of the monologue is a reminder that skull lights in Beckett's theater tend not stay out for long.

Rockaby (1979–80), first performed at the State University of New York's Buffalo campus, and *Ohio Impromptu* (1980), which premiered at Ohio State University, were written for seventy-fifth birthday celebrations for Beckett. In *Rockaby,* a spotlight shines on a prematurely old, white-faced woman wearing a lacy black evening gown and an extravagant headdress sitting on an otherwise dark stage in the rocking chair where her old mother rocked incessantly before her until she went crazy and died. Rocking, she listens for 15 minutes to her own voice issuing from a tape. Except for the woman's four utterances of "More," which activate the recording, the poetically fragmented text, with its echoing refrain, "time she stopped / *time she stopped,*" is entirely taped. The ending to *Rockaby* is harsh even for Beckett's theater. The crude brevity of the "fuck life" that breaks the repetitive rhythm of the last lines and is aimed perhaps at the memory of the woman's mother is a brutal condensation of Vladimir's "Astride a grave and a difficult birth." *Ohio Impromptu* adds two more white-haired old men to Beckett's repertory: L (listener) and R (reader), who reads, like the man he is reading about, "the sad tale through again" until "the sad tale a last time told. . . . Nothing is left to tell."

Beckett's "sad tale" had almost been "a last time told" in dramatic form. He wrote only a few more brief plays before his death in 1989. One of them, *Catastrophe* (1982), was written in honor of the persecuted Czechoslovakian playwright and political dissident Vaclav Havel. In *What Where,* written in French about 1983, four matching gray-haired clown figures, Bam, Bem, Bim, and Bom, dressed in identical long gray robes, enter and exit in geometric patterns when prodded by a fifth "character," V (Bam's voice). The last words are a characteristic condensation of Beckett's recurring challenge to audiences: "That is all. / Make sense who may. / I switch off" (*SP,* 316).

Da Capo

At the end of *Proust,* Beckett describes the musical convention of the da capo ("from the beginning") as "a testimony to the intimate and ineffable nature of an art that is perfectly intelligible and perfectly inexplicable" (*P,* 71). For most of Beckett's audiences and readers from the time of *Waiting for Godot*'s premiere, his plays, taking the same themes back to the beginning over and over again, have also seemed somehow both perfectly intelligible and perfectly inexplicable. More printed pages have been devoted to exploration of the inexplicable in Beckett, especially *Godot,* than to any other twentieth-century playwright. In 1929 Beckett said of *Finnegans Wake:* "Here is direct expression—pages and pages of it. And if you don't understand it, Ladies and Gentlemen, it is because you are too decadent to receive it. You are not satisfied unless form is so strictly divorced from content that you can comprehend the one almost without bothering to read the other" ("Dante," 26). Beckett went on to teach audiences to read form as content for 60 years, making fewer and fewer concessions to the "decadence" of the audience. He has been the most influential of the absurdist playwrights. Harold Pinter, Tom Stoppard, Sam Shepard, and David Mamet are among the many who acknowledge artistic debts to Beckett.[29] In a festschrift for Beckett's sixtieth birthday Fernando Arrabal wrote, "We too, the writers of today, have learnt to write thanks to Beckett. . . . The sensitive reality which he describes surrounds us and proclaims the necessity of the prodigious."[30]

Chapter Four

Eugène Ionesco

Eugène Ionesco is the closest in spirit to Dada and surrealism of the absurdist playwrights. "All that remains for me to do," he wrote in his memoirs, "is to give the lie to each spoken word by taking it apart, by making it explode, by transfiguring it."[1] His theater does not have the thematic richness of Beckett's. Ionesco's best dramatic work is explosively verbal, not cerebral, and makes an immediate, violent physical impact. Tragicomic, hallucinatory words and images rip the facade of convention from society's most comfortably familiar settings, the living room after dinner, for example, or a lesson, or the theater. In his prescription for what he called "anti-plays" Ionesco echoed Jarry and Artaud: "In the last resort drama is a revelation of monstrosity or of some monstrous formless state of being or of monstrous forms that we carry within ourselves" (*NCN,* 181).

Ionesco's career as a playwright began in almost impossibly limited material conditions and was subject to some of the most derogatory critical treatment accorded any of the "new theater." Nevertheless, in just 10 years, from 1950 to 1960, his situation evolved from parading with a sandwich board to entice spectators to buy a ticket for *The Bald Soprano* to having *Rhinoceros* performed at the prestigious Odéon Theater. By 1966, with plays in five theaters, Ionesco had become the most performed playwright in Paris. Today the tiny Left Bank Théâtre de la Huchette, where *The Bald Soprano* and *The Lesson* have been playing without interruption since 1957, has become something of a pilgrimage site for students and tourists curious to relive an early moment of the theater of the absurd. *The Bald Soprano* is still performed there as it was originally staged by Nicolas Bataille in 1950 with Jacques Noël's original decor and costumes.[2] Today, however, long ticket lines form outside the box office, a marked contrast to a May 1950 performance with only three people in the audience—one of Ionesco's early supporters, Ionesco's wife, and a passerby taking refuge from the cold.[3]

Background

Ionesco's theater is anchored in a preoccupation with the limits and vulnerability of language, a somewhat exaggerated determination to remain beyond ideology and politics, and an obsession with separation, loss, and death. It grew out of "the experience of being lost in the world, separated, lost in language and in my own language that I no longer felt to be mine but rather that of others" (*PP,* 169). He was born in Slatina, Romania, on 26 November 1912, to a French mother and a Romanian father. When he was 18 months old the family moved to Paris, where he remained with his mother and sister until he was 13. In 1916 his father returned to Romania, where Ionesco was forced to join him in 1925. Thus Ionesco's formative memories and linguistic development took shape in a context of exile and rupture. In *Découvertes* (Discoveries), he describes being overwhelmed by a feeling of monstrosity and alienation at a young age: "I looked in the mirror and I saw that I was naked, that is I saw that I was different, that I was not the others, that I was not like the others. Between me and the others, there was an infinite abyss. . . . I was isolated in my unlikeness, closed in by walls of difference that surrounded me, invisible but impenetrable, insurmountable walls that climbed to the sky."[4]

There was, however, one significant paradisiacal hiatus in Ionesco's childhood. Just after World War I, he was sent to a tiny rural village to become more robust. During the two years he spent in the country, he experienced a rare sense of belonging, moments of intense fullness and jubilation, luminous mornings, and "fortifying colors with a freshness and intensity they would never have again."[5] The experience left a stamp on Ionesco's remarkably visual approach to theater and constituted one end of the trajectory of the wildly swinging emotional pendulum that creates the basic pattern of his dramatic universe. "All my plays," he explained, "have their origin in two fundamental states of consciousness. . . . an awareness of evanescence and of solidity, of emptiness and of too much presence, of the unreal transparency of the world and its opacity, of light and of thick darkness" (*NCN,* 162).

In 1925 Ionesco's father, who had forged papers to obtain a divorce and had remarried, used his influence as a lawyer and former chief of police to obtain custody of his son. The 13-year-old Ionesco was forced to return to a father he came to abhor, a stepmother who disliked him, a language he did not know, and a country increasingly in the grip of fascism. Of his father, who managed to thrive during both the Nazi and Communist regimes in Romania, Ionesco later wrote, "Everything that I have done was done more or less against him. . . . He wanted me to become a bourgeois, a magistrate, a soldier, a chemical engineer. I was horrified by prosecuting attorneys; I couldn't lay eyes on a judge without wanting to kill him. I couldn't set eyes on an officer, a captain shod in boots, without giving way to fits of anger and despair. Everything that represented authority seemed to me, and is, unjust" (*PP*, 16–17). Urged by his father to study law, Ionesco chose to study French literature at the University of Bucharest. His degree finished, he wrote "surrealizing" poetry, taught French, and outraged Bucharest literary circles with nonconformist literary criticism. In 1938 he returned to Paris with his wife to write a thesis, never completed, on the themes of sin and death in modern French poetry. The outbreak of World War II interrupted their stay, but they were able to escape permanently to France in 1939.

With the almost accidental creation of *The Bald Soprano* in 1949, Ionesco, who had previously insisted that he did not like theater, began to write plays at a prodigious rate. In addition to some 20 major plays, several short sketches, and film scenarios, Ionesco published short stories (many of which became plays), several volumes of literary and polemical essays, journals, and memoirs. He also wrote children's tales and even dialogues for a French textbook for American students reflecting his absurd experience with the English language manual that prompted the creation of *The Bald Soprano*: "Perhaps," he suggested, "with these dialogues and monologues, the Americans won't learn French either."[6]

Anti-Plays: From *The Bald Soprano* to *Amédée*

Ionesco called his first play an "anti-play," a label that fits all his early theater. Like Flaubert, whom he much admired, and the Dada productions of his fellow Romanian Tristan Tzara, Ionesco attacked the language and logic of a society that buries meaning in clichés, propaganda, empty phrases, and abusive slogans. He also shared their defiant black humor. Dialogue shatters into fragments of sound and logic, which the characters hurl at one another with tragicomic consequences. The linguistic breakdown sweeps in its destructive path linear plots and three-dimensional characters. Ionesco, who spent hours as a child transfixed in front of the Punch-and-Judy shows in the Luxembourg Gardens, peoples his theater with violent Guignolesque figures.

La Cantatrice chauve (The Bald Soprano) Ionesco has described many times how the process of copying phrases from a manual he was using to learn English led to *The Bald Soprano:* "I found, reading them over attentively, that I was learning not English but some very surprising truths: that there are seven days in the week, for example, which I happened to know before; or that the floor is below us, the ceiling above us. . . . To my great surprise Mrs. Smith informed her husband that they had several children, that they lived in the outskirts of London, that their name was Smith, that Mr. Smith worked in an office, that they had a maid called Mary, who was English too" (*NCN,* 175–76). This humorous revelation of "fundamental truths" led Ionesco to the more anguished discovery that the "ready-made expressions and the most thread-bare clichés" of the language instruction manual were symptomatic of "all that is automatic in the language and behavior of people . . . the absence of any life within" (*NCN,* 180).

The initial stage directions for *The Bald Soprano,* which are sometimes read aloud at the beginning of the play, contain the adjective "English" 17 times and set in motion an erratic "English clock" that "strikes seventeen English strokes." Ionesco's Mr. Smith is seated in an "English armchair," wearing "English slippers," and reading an "English newspaper."[7] Mrs. Smith, who is darning "English socks," fires Ionesco's opening antitheater salvo, announcing: "There, it's nine o'clock. We've drunk the soup, and eaten the fish and chips, and the English salad. The children have drunk English water. We've eaten well this evening. That's because we live in the suburbs of London and because our name is Smith" (*FP,* 9). The exaggeratedly noncommittal Mr. Smith simply clucks his tongue very loudly. An obituary notice for a Bobby Watson unleashes a fantastic rapid-fire exchange about a family in which every member, male or female, is named Bobby Watson, and all are traveling salesmen. At one point, the name Bobby Watson occurs 22 times in 19 lines of text. Proliferation of nonsense is basic to Ionesco's antitheater: "By plunging into banality, by draining the sense from the hollowest clichés of everyday language . . . I tried to render the strangeness that seems to pervade our whole existence" (*NCN,* 28).

The Smiths are interrupted by the arrival of Mr. and Mrs. Martin. They rush off to change clothes, clearing the stage for a long, wildly parodical recognition scene during which the Martins deduce from the fact that they have taken the same train, live in the same house in the same city, sleep in the same bed, and have a daughter with one white eye and one red one that they must be husband and wife. When the Martins fall asleep in the same armchair, the Smiths' maid, Mary, no more fooled by logic than her creator, tiptoes back on stage to inform the audience that the Martins are not, after all, husband and wife. Mr. Martin's daughter's right eye is white, whereas Mrs. Martin's daughter's white eye is her left one.

The Smiths return wearing the same clothes. Much throat clearing and a long hostile silence, as uncomfortable for the spectators as for the Smiths and the Martins, precedes a vacuous conversation, which is interrupted by the doorbell. Three times Mrs. Smith goes to the door in response to the bell but finds no one. Angrily deducing that "experience teaches us that when one hears the doorbell ring, it is because there is never anyone there," she is immediately contradicted by Mr. Smith, who then answers a fourth ring and admits a fire chief who reluctantly entertains them with "moral fables" and a convoluted family epic entitled "The Head Cold." When he departs, thanked by Mrs. Martin for "a truly Cartesian quarter of an hour," he asks about the Bald Soprano. His inquiry is greeted with awkward silence broken by the embarrassed reply that she is still wearing her hair the same way.[8]

Paced by the accelerating rhythm of the erratic clock, the inanely platitudinous conversation, much of it taken verbatim from the English language manual, degenerates into savage linguistic anarchy. As the stage lights are extinguished, the screaming Smiths and Martins are mechanically hurling insults and meaningless chants. The lights come back on almost immediately and the play starts over. In the first performances, the Smiths reappeared in their living room. Later, Ionesco substituted the Martins for the Smiths to emphasize the empty interchangeability of these puppetlike figures: "The Smiths and the Martins no longer know how to talk because they no longer know how to think, they no longer know how to think because they are no longer capable of being moved, they have no passions, they no longer know how to be, they can become anyone or anything, for they are no longer themselves, in an impersonal world, they can only be someone else, they are interchangeable" (*NCN,* 180).

Ionesco's language in *The Bald Soprano* has been described as "a sort of deadly lullaby that perverts the function of language."[9] The perversion of language in Ionesco's theater was not an end in itself, however. Like the surrealists, he attacked the stillborn language of cliché and propaganda in an attempt to replace it with one that would be alive with magic possibilities. *The Bald Soprano* had a one-month run in 1950 in front of rows of empty seats.

La Leçon (The Lesson) Words again go out of control in *The Lesson* (1950), leading to an orgy of philological aggression that culminates in a sadistic murder. While the spoken words float comically at the surface of the action, a physical transformation of the pupil and professor communicates the violence and degradation that festers in the parodical text of the lesson. The initially polite, if excitable and ridiculously self-effacing, professor turns into a lewd tyrant while the 18-year-old pupil, who is remarkably lively and outgoing when she arrives, becomes "almost a mute and inert object" (*FP,* 45–46).

The lesson begins with arithmetic. The pupil can count to infinity and solve preposterously difficult multiplication problems, but she is unable to subtract, causing the professor to warn prophetically: "It's not enough to integrate, you must also disintegrate. That's the way life is. That's philosophy. That's science. That's progress, civilization" (*FP,* 55). Abandoning his increasingly impertinent "word problems," along with the pupil's comical hopes for the "total doctorate," he delivers a farcically overblown lecture on the "linguistic and comparative philology of the neo-Spanish languages." As the professor speaks, Ionesco exposes the hollowness of language, inflating it like an empty balloon. "If you utter several sounds at an accelerated speed," the professor informs his pupil, "they will automatically cling to each other, constituting thus syllables, words, even sentences, that is to say groupings of various importance, purely irrational assemblages of sounds, denuded of all sense, but for that very reason the more capable of maintaining themselves without danger at high altitude in the air" (*FP,* 62–63).

Infuriated by the increasingly disinterested pupil's complaints about a toothache, the professor fulfills his maid's prophesy that "philology leads to calamity." Wielding a knife, he circles the pupil in a kind of scalp dance while she feebly describes pains in her throat, neck, shoulders, breasts, thighs, and hips. When he stabs her, she falls into a chair with her legs spread immodestly. The stage directions indicate that the cries and the rhythm of their movements must emphasize the orgiastic nature of the knifing for both pupil and professor. Ionesco particularly admired a performance of *The Lesson* during which the shadows of the characters projected against a wall brought out an element of ritual savagery he had not foreseen: "It was more than a rape, it was vampirism. . . . As the action moved along, he devoured the girl, he drank her blood. And while he became stronger and stronger, she lost her vitality" (*VR,* 104). The professor and the maid, who returns to scold him for what turns out to be his fortieth murder, exit with the body.[10] For a few moments, the stage remains disturbingly empty, just as it was at the beginning of the play, and then the forty-first pupil rings the doorbell.

As in *The Bald Soprano,* the substitution of a cyclical structure for psychological development underscores an apparently endless mechanical cycle of violence. The accelerating rhythm of the verbal attacks, which unleash the sexual aggressions of the professor (while reducing the pupil to an almost moronic passivity), gives the minimal plot its deadly momentum. *The Lesson* is subtitled "A Comic Drama." Ionesco refused to recognize traditional distinctions between comedy and tragedy: "As the 'comic' is an intuitive perception of the absurd, it seems to me more hopeless than the 'tragic.' The 'comic' offers no escape" (*NCN,* 27). This is an effective piece of theater of cruelty. The nonsensical wordplay makes the brutality all the more shocking. Outraged spectators at a 1951 performance in Brussels demanded refunds for their tickets. The actor who played the professor had to flee through a secret door.[11]

Jacques, ou la soumission (Jack; or, The Submission)* and *L'Avenir est dans les oeufs (The Future Is in Eggs) Ionesco described his next play, also written in 1950, as "a kind of parody or caricature of boulevard theatre . . . going bad, gone mad" (*NCN,* 194). Subtitled "A Naturalistic Comedy," *Jack* is really a surrealist farce. The hero, Jack, has green hair. His first marriage prospect, the two-nosed Roberta I, has "green pimples on her beige skin, red breasts on a mauve background, an illuminated navel, a tongue the color of tomato sauce, pan-browned square shoulders, and all the meat needed to merit the highest commendation" (*FP,* 91–92). Her replacement, Roberta II, has three noses and a nine-fingered hand. All the characters but the rebellious Jack, "naked" in his difference as Ionesco described himself as a child in *Découvertes,* wear masks. Jack's mother, father, sister, and grandparents, reminiscent of the Bobby Watsons, are all named Jack. Comic volleys of malapropisms, neologisms, warped clichés and slogans, provocative sounds, and distorted historical and literary references are fired at Jack as he is manipulated into filial submission. Jack remains silent and unyielding until, lamenting, "Oh words, what crimes are committed in your name," he is confronted with the terrifying fact that he is "chronometrable" and surrenders (*FP,* 86). The exultant family immediately produces Roberta I, veiled and in bridal array, flanked by her *Ubu*esque parents, the Roberts. When Jack refuses to marry her because she has only two noses, the Roberts produce Roberta II, a second "only daughter" with the requisite three noses, played by the same actress that plays Roberta I.

Jack, who resembles Vitrac's Victor, tells Roberta that he has been a victim of a cruel precocity and of deceiving adults. She recites a dream about a burning stallion while a blazing horse's mane crosses from one end of the stage to the other. As the rhythm of her speech accelerates to a gallop, Jack picks up the frenzied recital until he becomes himself the burning stallion, exhausted and thirsty. Caught in Roberta's dream, Jack is seduced into submissive adulthood by the englobing dampness of her earthy sexual imagery: "I'm moist. . . . My necklace is made of mud, my breasts are dissolving, my pelvis is wet, I've got water in my crevasses, I'm sinking down. My true name is Liza. In my belly, there are pools, swamps. . . . I've got a house of clay" (*FP,* 107–8). The seduction scene is bathed in a phantasmagoric greenish light contrasting with the drab gray of the family scenes. At the end of the play, all the other Jacks and Roberts, squatting and making obscene animal noises, encircle the embracing Jack and Roberta, who are playing a word game in which all language is reduced to "cat." Ionesco's long note for this scene directs that "this must produce in the audience a feeling of embarrassment, awkwardness and shame" (*FP,* 110).

Jack is the first of Ionesco's plays constructed from clearly autobiographical elements. Echoing Ionesco's adolescent experience in Romania, Jack tells Roberta: "When I was born, I was almost fourteen years old. That's why I was able to understand more easily than most what it was all about. . . . everything was fake. . . . Ah, they had lied to me. . . . they all had the word goodness in their mouths, a bloody knife between their teeth" (*FP,* 103–4). The oneiric excursions are based on actual dreams recorded by Ionesco in his journals. After *Jack,* Ionesco used dream material in nearly every one of his major plays. The explicitly sexual nature of *Jack* kept it from the stage until 1955, when Robert Postec staged it along with Ionesco's short sketch *Le Tableau* (The Picture) at the Théâtre de la Huchette, where its reception was mixed.

In *The Future Is in Eggs* (1951), a circuslike sequel to *Jack,* Jack and Roberta, still chanting "cat" and locked in their embrace, are once again surrounded by all the Jacks and Roberts, who accuse them of neglecting their reproductive duties. The play ends with a clucking Roberta producing basketful after basketful of eggs. Crying, "Long live the white race," the triumphant families dump them on Jack, who is sitting on a hatching machine. The invasion of the stage by proliferating objects, the "materialization of solitude" according to Ionesco, became a hallmark of his theater, where characters are as frequently buried in objects as in words. In *Le Nouveau locataire* (*The New Tenant*), written in 1953, the main character is finally suffocated by his belongings.

Les Chaises (The Chairs) In his program notes for the first production of *The Chairs* in 1952, Ionesco wrote, "As the world is incomprehensible to me, I am waiting for someone to explain it" (*NCN,* 186). In the play that wait is assigned to a 95-year-old man and his 94-year-old spouse, Semiramis, a wife-mother figure with sagging stockings, sinking petticoats, and the name of a legendary queen of Assyria and Babylonia. They await the arrival of an orator who will deliver the old man's message to mankind and give meaning to an existence as empty as it has been long. To pass the time as they wait in their isolated lodging, a kind of caretaker's apartment in a tower surrounded by the sea, the old couple rehashes the same anecdotes and plays the same charades, word games, and infantile role reversals that have been their weapons against the void for some 75 years. Their routine is interrupted by the sound of a boat and the ringing of the doorbell announcing the first of a host of invisible guests invited by the old man to hear the orator.

Unlike the doorbell episode in *The Bald Soprano,* the invisible guests who ring the bell in *The Chairs* are meant to be very real presences. Fearing that the spectators might interpret the invisible characters "in the usual dull way, psychologically or rationally," and dismiss them as simply the memories or remorse of the senile old couple, Ionesco wanted them to seem much more real than the orator (*NCN,* 190). Each is realistically welcomed by the chatty, flirtatious old man and provided a real chair by the increasingly frantic old woman, who races on- and offstage procuring seats for each arrival while she also hawks Eskimo pies like a seasoned pro and coquettishly lifts her bedraggled petticoats and bares her breasts. "The chairs," Ionesco explained, "coming at great speed and at an accelerating rate . . . expressed for me the ontological emptiness, a sort of whirlwind of emptiness" (*VR,* 82). By the time the emperor arrives unexpectedly, sending the surprised old man into a fit of barking, lamentations, and frenzied panegyrics, the stage is filled with empty chairs blocking the old man and woman against opposite walls. Pathetically separated but puerilely confident that the message will be delivered, they leap into the sea when the orator finally appears, with their illusions of dying "in full glory . . . in order to become a legend," or at least having a street named after them, still intact (*FP,* 158). Signing to the audience that he is a deafmute, the orator makes a few desperate and incomprehensible sounds, writes gibberish on a blackboard, and finally departs through doors opened onto blackness. The audience must confront what the old couple has finally escaped: the "meaninglessness and arbitrariness, the vacuity of reality, language and human thought" (*NCN,* 188).

Talking constantly and mechanically echoing each other in surrealist collages of fragmented thoughts and distorted maxims laced with the refrain "if only," the old man and woman, like Beckett's garrulous couples, bear out the old man's observation that "the further one goes, the deeper one sinks. It's because the earth keeps turning around, around, around, around" (*FP,* 114). The old man has an intuition of salvation by means of a fragile silence: "Sometimes I awaken in the midst of absolute silence. It's a perfect circle. There's nothing lacking. But one must be careful, all the same. Its shape might disappear. There are holes through which it can escape" (*FP,* 145). As in Beckett's theater, however, the human voice goes wretchedly on. Even the deafmute orator makes desperate noises.

The Chairs marks a giant step in Ionesco's mastery of stage language.

The effect of the spoken word is more physical than mental, choreographed into a berserk dance mirrored by the acrobatics of the hobbling Semiramis. Carefully orchestrated light effects play a major role. The lighting of a gas lamp in the opening moments, dispelling a ghostly half-light, creates an oneiric green light like that used for *Jack,* evocative of both the surrounding sea and the musty light of old dreams and deceptions. When the front doors crash open announcing the arrival of the emperor, a powerful but "cold empty light" floods the stage. Ionesco suggested that the bright light be extinguished with the exit of the orator: "At this moment the audience would have in front of them, bathed in a light that is once again dim and ghostly as at the beginning of the play . . . empty chairs on an empty stage decorated with streamers, littered with useless confetti, which would give an impression of sadness, emptiness and disenchantment such as one finds in a ballroom after a dance" (*NCN,* 191).

The initial production in 1952, to which Adamov came night after night to applaud in a nearly empty theater, was a failure. In 1956, however, a revival by Jacques Mauclair won an important prize and inspired an enthusiastic review by Jean Anouilh, which helped make Ionesco famous. Anouilh compared *The Chairs* to Molière "because it's black in a perfectly droll manner, horrible and comical, poignant and always true."[12] *The Chairs* is still considered by many to be Ionesco's finest play.

Victimes du devoir (Victims of Duty) In *Victims,* a "Pseudodrama" written in 1952, the eschewal of a logical, linear plot and psychological development represents more than dramatic terrorism. The erratic time sequences and oneiric instability of character are patterned after a psychoanalytic investigation. At the beginning of the play, the main character, Choubert, observes to his skeptical wife, Madeleine, "All the plays that have ever been written, from Ancient Greece to the present day, have never really been anything but thrillers. Drama's always been realistic and there's always been a detective about."[13] His opinion is comically affirmed by the appearance of a shy young detective seeking information about a previous tenant named Mallot or Mallod. When Choubert volunteers that the name ends in *t,* the detective is suddenly transformed into a familiar protean figure in Ionesco's theater. He becomes a father figure, a caricature of a fascist policeman doubling as a psychoanalyst, who forces Choubert into a painfully mimed descent into his psyche, where he is to exhume his memories of Mallot.

Madeleine undergoes an equally dramatic metamorphosis. Returning from her kitchen with a new walk and a musical voice—her dress falls away to reveal a much sexier one—she becomes the detective's lover and accomplice.[14] Telling Choubert to loosen his legs and hold tight to the handrail represented by her extended arm, she guides him down. As he fights his way through his memories, Madeleine plays the roles of his mother and lover opposite the detective-father. Choubert's memories are Ionesco's. Madeleine threatens to poison herself during a quarrel with the detective as Ionesco's mother had once done in his presence. Choubert wrings his hands during the quarrel, muttering, "Father, mother, father, mother" (*ATV,* 134). The exchanges between Choubert and the detective echo the painful cycle of accusations and ineffective reconciliation attempts between Ionesco and his father.

Choubert briefly escapes their tyranny. A series of contradictory experiences of "joy and pain" and "fullness and emptiness," mimed as a long, difficult journey to the summit of a mountain, leads to a momentary lightness of being. When he plunges back to reality, he falls into a wastebasket. To punish Choubert, who has not found Mallot, and fill the gaps in his memory, the detective pulls a huge crust of bread from his briefcase and begins mechanically stuffing bread into the weeping Choubert's mouth while Madeleine, just as mechanically, goes faster and faster in and out of the kitchen placing cups of coffee on the sideboard until the entire sideboard is buried under piles of cups. A poet friend, Nicolas d'Eu, stabs the detective after a long speech delivered in apparent oblivion to Choubert's suffering, calling for a "surrealizing" revolutionary theater: "We'll get rid of the principle of identity and unity of character and let movement and dynamic psychology take its place. . . . As for plot and motivation. . . . We ought to ignore them completely, at least in their old form, which was too clumsy, too obvious" (*ATV,* 158–59). The detective dies, crying, "Long live the white race," and maintaining that he is a victim of his duty. Even then the mechanical brutality does not stop. Madeleine and Nicolas d'Eu, whose name rhymes comically with that of the Russian emperor parodied by Jarry in *Ubu,* take over. As the play ends they are all chewing and claiming, even Choubert with his mouth full, to be victims of duty.

The stuffing of Choubert is the kind of multifaceted image that keeps Ionesco's theater uniquely hilarious and horrifying. A playful allusion to the original meaning of farce, it is also a vivid physical metaphor for the stifling brutality of paternal and fascist manipulation experienced by Ionesco and for the filial guilt that haunted him. When Jacques Mauclair staged *Victims* in 1953, his use of pantomime to capture the surrealistic mining of Choubert's psyche, particularly the scene where Choubert makes his fantastically far-flung imaginary voyage across oceans and forests and up the mountain, was for Ionesco an important revelation of the fundamentally physical nature of theater. "I understood what theater . . . was meant to be: a living experience, real, not just the illustration of a text. . . . it was theater because it was at the same time true and false" (*VR,* 97).

Amédée, ou Comment s'en débarasser (Amédée; or, How to Get Rid of It) In *Amédée* (1953), Ionesco's first three-act play, the central figure is again a couple. Amédée, a dreamy playwright nursing a writer's block, is another character used by Ionesco to explode conventional psychology and the comforting western myth of individuality. One third of the people in Paris, he explains, refusing to accept a letter from the mailman, have the same name. His nagging, exaggeratedly housewifely spouse, another Madeleine, works as a switchboard operator from their combination living room–office, shifting from one role to the other with a ritualized exchange of her apron for a hat. In many ways, they are among the most realistically portrayed of Ionesco's couples, arguing over Amédée's drinking, the household budget, and the inequitable distribution of labor, but their ordinariness is a foil to "what is unusual, strange or symbolic" (*VR,* 83). What is most immediately strange and symbolic in the life of Amédée and Madeleine is that they have poisonous mushrooms sprouting in their living room and have been isolated in their apartment for 15 years because there is an enormous corpse with great shining green eyes in their bedroom. Although they argue over who is to blame, neither Amédée nor Madeleine can remember why the corpse is there. Toward the end of the play, when he has escaped from the apartment, Amédée explains to a drunken American soldier, "It's a great misfortune, the tragedy of our life . . . the skeleton in our cupboard" (*ATV,* 68). The growing corpse is a symbol of remorse and also a measure of the abyss of misunderstanding that separates Ionesco's symbolic couple.

During the first two acts, the cadaver, which had been confined to their bedroom, begins to grow at a terrifying rate. It erupts on stage, enormous feet first, nearly burying Amédée and Madeleine in their furniture. Fear that it will push through to the landing and alert the already suspicious neighbors finally rouses the eternally fatigued Amédée to get rid of it. As he awaits his midnight excursion he tugs on an invisible rope, pulling out an image of his youth. A matching set of actors enters from the back of the stage portraying Amédée as a young bridegroom and Madeleine in her bridal veil. Amédée II speaks of warmth and light, freedom and love. A fearful Madeleine II rejects his sexual overtures, shrieking of pain, damp darkness, and deception. As their words and worlds grow farther apart, their language collapses into a meaningless crisscross of rhymes and repetitions until a screaming Madeleine II rushes off the stage.

Making a superhuman effort, Amédée pulls the massive corpse through the window. When the body finally yields, the stage directions call for the whole set to tremble in a tremendous crash of furniture and falling plaster, giving the impression that the corpse "is dragging the whole house with it and tugging at the entrails of the two principal characters" (*ATV,* 62). Amédée descends with it into an astonishingly beautiful moonlit night. As he struggles toward the river, the gigantic corpse suddenly opens out like a great sail or parachute. Amédée drifts up to freedom, escaping his burden of guilt and, more immediately, eluding Madeleine and the police, who are pursuing him. Exceptionally in Ionesco's theater, Amédée does not fall.

The staging of *Amédée* helped clarify for Ionesco an idea of theater he had been grappling with from the beginning: "The foundation of a comedy of language, this state of astonishment or of dreaming before a reality that becomes disjointed, that breaks up, I accomplished it . . . with the cadaver that grows, that one sees, that one no longer sees, that vanishes" (*VR,* 93). Although the reviews were mixed, *Amédée* was compared favorably by several critics to Beckett's *Waiting for Godot*. Ionesco was being taken much more seriously as a playwright.

Polemics

Initially the harshest attacks on Ionesco's theater came from conservative critics. By the mid-1950s, however, Ionesco, who maintained that "all committed writers seek to violate you," was embroiled in a conflict with critics on the left that centered on his refusal to take a political stance in his theater.[15] The most famous of his anti-ideological skirmishes pitted Ionesco against Kenneth Tynan, the drama critic for the *London Observer,* who had been an early supporter of Ionesco. After seeing a performance of *The Chairs,* Tynan objected to "that bleak new world from which the humanist heresies of faith in logic and belief in man will be forever be banished." He dismissed Ionesco's theater as "a funfair ride on a ghost train . . . from which we emerge into the far more intimidating clamor of diurnal reality." Ionesco accused Tynan of acknowledging "only one plane of reality: what is called the 'social' plane, which seems to me to be the most external, in other words the most superficial" (*NCN,* 89–91).

In 1955 Ionesco wrote a Molièresque satire attacking both Brechtian and Sartrean notions of engaged theater, *L'Impromptu d'Alma, ou le caméleon berger* (*Improvisation; or, The Shepherd's Chameleon*). *Improvisa-*

tion pits Ionesco against his critics, cast as three Guignolesque pedants: Bartholomeus I, II, and III, doctors of decorology, costumitude, and spectatopsychology. At the end of the play, the character playing Ionesco pronounces a serious dramatic credo reflecting Ionesco's growing interest in Jung: "For me the theatre is the projection onto the stage of the world within: it is in my dreams, my anguish, my dark desires, my inner contradictions that I reserve the right to find the stuff of my plays."[16] In the next phase of his dramatic career, Ionesco drew even more heavily on dreams and memories. He also became increasingly preoccupied with politics but not in a way that endeared him to liberal critics.

The Bérenger Plays

In 1957 Ionesco created the first of a series of comically pathetic Everyman figures named Bérenger who, in their various incarnations, became the main characters in his next four major plays: *Tueur sans gages* (*The Killer*), *Rhinoceros, Le Piéton de l'air* (*A Stroll in the Air*), and *Le Roi se meurt* (*Exit the King*). The Bérengers, who combine the dreamily ineffective bravado of Charlie Chaplin with the angst and political concerns of their creator, share Ionesco's inability to resign himself to the human condition. "I have never quite succeeded," Ionesco confessed, "in getting used to existence, whether it be the existence of the world or other people, or above all myself" (*NCN,* 157). The Bérenger plays inaugurated a new phase in Ionesco's theater. Surrealist roots are still apparent in the increasingly fantastic stage effects, but the more serious tone, sustained plots, and almost autobiographical characters are closer to Kafka's world than the verbal warfare of the "anti-plays." Two of the Bérenger plays are among the most important in Ionesco's theater. *Rhinoceros* is his best-known play; *Exit the King* contends with *The Chairs* for being his finest.

Tueur sans gages (The Killer)* and *Rhinoceros The first of the Bérenger plays, *The Killer* (1957), is a biting denunciation of herd psychology and ideologically manipulative language. One of the characters, a demagogic keeper of geese named Mother Peep, enthralls her goose-stepping fellow citizens by proclaiming that "to disalienate mankind, we must alienate each individual man" (*K,* 77). She promises that "if an ideology doesn't apply to real life, we'll say it does and it'll all be perfect. The intellectuals will back us up. They'll find us anti-myths to set against the old ones. We'll replace the myths . . . by slogans . . . and the latest platitudes" (*K,* 80). *The Killer* unfolds in the illogical spatial and temporal dimensions of a nightmare. At the end of the play, Bérenger is alone on a darkening stage trapped in a phantasmagoric slow motion. The stage directions indicate that he is to give the impression of walking a long time without advancing as the decor begins to disappear. Caught in the empty darkness, which underscores the barrenness of his words, he confronts the killer and unsuccessfully attempts to disarm him with a cliché-ridden monologue. Once more in Ionesco's theater, reified language leads to devastating consequences.

Rhinoceros, a three-act play written in 1958, began as an anti-Nazi play but broadened into a denunciation of "all the collective hysterias and the epidemics that hide under the cover of reason and ideas."[17] The play was based on a short story written the previous year by Ionesco, inspired by his reading of Kafka. The term *rhinoceritis* had appeared frequently in Ionesco's journals long before, however. "Imagine," he wrote in 1941, "that one fine morning you discover that rhinoceroses have taken power. They have a rhinoceros ethics, a rhinoceros philosophy, a rhinoceros universe" (*PP,* 67).

Rhinoceros begins on a Sunday afternoon on the terrace of a provincial café, where a hungover Bérenger is being barraged with "humanizing" suggestions by his friend Jean, who touts himself as a "superior man who fulfills his duty." Echoing his author, Bérenger excuses his apathy by explaining: "I feel out of place in life. . . . I can't seem to get used to myself."[18] His alienation suddenly takes concrete form when the Sunday quiet is broken by what seem to be rhinoceroses racing by in a cloud of dust. The initial surprise of the other characters witnessing the event quickly degenerates into a hostile argument about the nature of the rhinoceroses, temporarily resolved by the absurd logic of a straw-hatted, card-carrying logician.

The argument about the rhinoceroses resumes in the next scene, at the legal publishing house where Jean is a clerk. In their stubborn illogicality or overeagerness to reach a consensus, all the employees but Daisy, the secretary with whom Bérenger is in love, and Bérenger, who sneaks into the office late, begin to show signs of incipient rhinoceritis. As they argue, the wife of an absent employee recognizes her plaintively bellowing spouse among the growing band of rhinoceroses charging about in the streets and leaps to join him. Bérenger goes to visit Jean and is alarmed to find his friend greenish, rough-voiced, and fretting over a bump on his forehead. Jean makes numerous trips to his bathroom, emerging each time with greener skin and a longer protrusion, until he too turns into a particularly nasty rhinoceros. Fleeing, Bérenger discovers that Jean's neighbors have also been transformed and that the streets have been taken over by rhinoceroses.

The final act takes place in Bérenger's room. Feverishly testing the surface of his forehead, around which he has tied a handkerchief to keep a horn from sprouting, Bérenger receives his colleague Dudard and then Daisy. Dudard succumbs to the epidemic, voicing, as Jean had earlier, perennial fascist excuses. Outside the window, a rhinoceros runs by, sporting the logician's straw hat. Determined to hold out, Bérenger and Daisy promise to sustain each other with love. They quarrel almost immediately, and Daisy joins the rhinoceroses. Bérenger weakens, but to his dismay is forced to recognize that he is incapable of becoming a rhinoceros: he can't speak their language, his skin won't thicken, and his voice won't change. Reacting with angry defiance, he cries out at the end of a long monologue: "I'm the last man left, and I'm staying that way until the end! I'm not capitulating" (*R,* 107).

Ionesco's experience in Romania, where he watched initially antifascist friends and respected professors succumb to fascism, had been a dreadful lesson about both the powerful appeal of joining the herd and the isolation of the individual who says no. His awareness of the possibility of the kind of gut-level, unheroic resistance represented by Bérenger, as opposed to some of the lofty ideological or moral stances of existentialism, gives *Rhinoceros* a human appeal. First staged in Düsseldorf in 1959, and then by Jean-Louis Barrault at the Odéon in 1960, *Rhinoceros* has had thousands of performances all over the world. Its immediate success was due in part to its accessible message and also to a growing acceptance of the theater of the absurd.

Rhinoceros is difficult to stage. Although Ionesco satirizes the degradation of language, logic, and morality with the same irreverent verve as in his early theater, the phenomenon of rhinoceritis must be made more tragic than comic and as convincingly real as it is patently fantastic. Staged clumsily, it becomes embarrassingly grotesque, and the tragic quality of the metaphor is destroyed. Ionesco faulted the successful Broadway production for making *Rhinoceros* simply funny and anticonformist. In 1960, at the Odéon Theater, Jean-Louis Barrault staged the metamorphoses concretely, using the comic effect as a conduit to a more subtle anguish. Other directors, eschewing props and stage machinery, have represented rhinoceritis as a strictly psychological state. Although *Rhinoceros* was an enormous success, many of the early champions of Ionesco's antitheater regretted its more classical form and the overt symbolism of its political message. A critic for *Le Monde* commented, "An enthusiast from the time of the catacombs has the right to deplore that after having brilliantly discovered the unusual in the banal, Ionesco has fallen . . . into the banality of the unusual and into the preaching symbolism that he detested."[19]

Le Piéton de l'air (A Stroll in Air)* and *Le Roi se meurt (Exit the King) *A Stroll in the Air* (1962), which was also staged by Barrault at the Odéon, is most remarkable for its fantastic stage effects. In its dreamlike landscapes a great silver bridge spans an imaginary abyss, pink ruins are smothered in flowers, and the Eiffel Tower makes a sudden appearance. A representative of the underworld floats on- and offstage. When Bérenger demonstrates the simplicity of flying, he takes flight on a magic white bicycle as the stage is suddenly transformed from the English countryside into a circus with acrobat's rings.

Insisting that to fly is natural and that man has lost his ability to do so because he has lost his sense of wonder, the third Bérenger floats off to an "anti-world," which he compares to "the sun's rays shining through a crystal prism . . . disintegrating into a patchwork of colors and then put together again."[20] Bérenger's flight is an Artaudian version of the swing from lightness to heaviness that shapes so many of Ionesco's plays. The antiworld turns out to be an apocalyptic nightmare of blood and destruction from which he returns exhausted and taciturn.

Described by Ionesco as a "dramatic fantasy . . . more a spectacle than a play or an anti play," *A Stroll* signals Ionesco's growing detachment from the provocative simplicity and rebelliousness of his antitheater.[21] Disappointed critics generally treated the play and its author harshly. That same year, however, Ionesco created *Exit the King,* a magnificent work that combines the verbal richness of his earlier theater and the poignancy of the various Bérengers' unresigned combat against the painful givens of the human condition. Ionesco, recovering from a serious illness, wrote the play, he said, that he might learn to die: "It was to be a lesson, a sort of spiritual exercise, a gradual progress, stage by stage towards the ineluctable end, which I tried to make accessible to other people" (*F,* 88). Originally entitled *La Cérémonie* (The Ceremony), it is a long, ritually paced one-act play.

Bérenger is a king in his last incarnation, credited with titles and epic feats of ludicrous grandiosity. Because he refuses to recognize after a reign spanning eons that "kings are only provisionally immortal," Marguerite, his first queen, is determined to teach him to die. "You're going to die in an hour and a half," the severe Marguerite informs him, "you're going to die at the end of the show."[22] Bérenger is determined to die "when I've got the time, when I make up my mind."[23] In an Ubuesque moment, he bargains with the sun to "let every creature die provided *I* can live forever" (*EK,* 52). From the moment Bérenger walks on stage, crown askew, he is bombarded by reminders that his time is up. His failing limbs, the source of a number of clowning pratfalls, presage the moment when he can no longer hold on to his beloved scepter. Great cracks in the walls of his palace and the complete breakdown of the central heating are symptomatic of a kingdom so worn out that it is pulling the entire universe in its destructive wake.[24] All that remains of his kingdom is his crumbling throne room; his two wives; the doctor; a comically dim-witted, garrulous guard; and his old nurse, Juliette. The stichomythic exchanges between Bérenger and Juliette—her lines a litany of life's accumulated miseries, his a belated paean to the sublimity of every lived moment—are a keen reminder that life, painful as it is, is all there is.

As the final moments approach, Bérenger's supporting cast disappears. He becomes blind and deaf to all but Marguerite, who, as wives so often do in Ionesco's theater, becomes a mother figure, "giving birth" to a Bérenger free to die. After cutting an imaginary cord with an invisible scissors, she mimes his release from the weight of the world, removing a ball and chain, a sack that was making him round-shouldered, a spare pair of army boots, a rifle, a machine gun, a rusty old saber, the thorns and splinters in his cloak, creepers, seaweed, and slimy, wet leaves. As the doors, walls, and windows of the throne room disappear, Marguerite leads him beyond the grasp of colors, sounds, and perfumes and finally to his throne. Marguerite disappears, leaving Bérenger, seated at last on his throne, alone on a stage bathed in a grayish light. After a few moments he slowly fades away into a mist. For the original production, Jacques Noël had the backdrops painted on the reverse side of the cloth and lighted from behind so the kingdom could be made to disappear into grayness at the end of Bérenger's performance by simply extinguishing the lights.[25]

Bérenger's clownlike lack of dignity, combined with the anguish of his appeal for immortality, re-creates the extraordinary synthesis of tragedy and comic triviality that Ionesco achieved in *The Chairs.* Like the Old Man and Semiramis, with whom they share a claustrophobic isolation and an astounding capacity for delusional anachronisms, Bérenger and his entourage are neither full-fledged psychological entities nor one-dimensional puppets. Falling somewhere in between, sometimes very fully human, sometimes grotesquely mechanical, they complete Ionesco's picture, begun in *The Chairs,* of human existence as a "whirlwind of emptiness." Audiences, becoming accustomed to the absurdist theater's treatment of serious issues in a fantastic and farcical vein, were more moved by *Exit the King* than shocked by it. "One laughs a lot," commented one critic, "a laughter that never succeeds in killing or even diminishing the anguishing impression of personal terror created by the descent toward his end of the old king."[26] *Exit the King* closes Ionesco's Bérenger cycle. In many respects, it also closes the chapter of Ionesco's absurd theater, at least insofar as that flexible concept is related to the explosion of conventional language and logic and parody of traditional theatrical stratagems.

La Soif et la faim (Hunger and Thirst)

After *Exit the King,* Ionesco acknowledged that he was moving away from the spirit of "Pataphysics" and caught himself "at the game of message bearing."[27] His post-Bérenger plays are generally more sober and brooding, increasingly focused on a personal message or quest, and more conventional in their dependence on rhetoric and technical paraphernalia. *Hunger and Thirst,* written in 1964, develops a theme that had long haunted Ionesco: "Ever since I became fully conscious of time I have felt old and I have wanted to live. I have run after life as though to catch time. . . . I have run after life so much that it has always escaped me" (*F,* 21). Jean, the Bérenger-like protagonist of *Hunger and Thirst,* is terrified by the rapid passage of time. He longs for sunlight and lightness of being and speaks with envy of people who "live on magical hilltops, glistening peaks" and pay absurdly low rents into the bargain.[28] During a game of hide-and-seek with his wife, he flees the trap of domesticity and a lifetime of remorse symbolized by a damp basement apartment and the appearance of a reproachful old aunt, dead for years.

In the long, hallucinatory final episode, which Ionesco called "The Black Mass of the Good Inn," a visibly aged and exhausted Jean arrives, after a long voyage marked by disappointments, at a sinister monastery-barracks-prison. The monks provide him copious servings of food, but he continues to be tormented by an unappeasable hunger and thirst. Subjected to a test on his adventures, Jean gets low marks for his disappointing answers. The interrogation is followed by an educational game, a spectacular brainwashing session during which two starving, caged clowns—Tripp, a religious man flanked by monks in black, and Brechtoll (obviously Ionesco's nemesis, Brecht), an atheist flanked by monks in red—are swung on stage and tortured with promises of food until they change roles. Tripp renounces God and Brechtoll recites a prayer. Attempting to leave, Jean requests his bill but discovers that the sum owed is as limitless as his unappeasable appetite. The monks have judged the tale of his travels too insignificant to be considered a fair exchange for their hospitality. During the negotiations, the back of the stage lights up, revealing beyond the bars of the monastery the kind of euphoric lightness that has evaded Jean. His wife and now 15-year-old daughter, who was only an infant when Jean struck out on his own, appear in a magically luminous garden. Waving and shouting "I'm coming," Jean is sentenced to feed the monastery's new arrivals until he has paid his astronomical debt. As the play ends, he is serving mechanically at an ever-accelerating pace while the monks chant the accountant's wildly multiplying figures which appear at first on a blackboard and then are flashed all about on screens that light up simultaneously on different parts of the stage.

A nightmarish evocation of the human incapacity for happiness and the apparent hopelessness of a search for meaning and truth, *Hunger and Thirst* is most successful as a visual extravaganza. It has neither the sustained, anguished tension nor the verbal dynamism of the earlier plays. Nevertheless, with *Hunger and Thirst,* the theater of the absurd joined the classics at the Comédie-Française in 1966.

Apocalyptic Visions

Ionesco's plays after *Hunger and Thirst* reflect an even darker, more foreboding vision of the human condition. His *L'Epidemie, ou Jeux de massacre* (*The Killing Game*), first staged by Jorge Lavelli in 1970, is a graphically violent play inspired by Daniel Defoe's *A Journal of the Plague Year.* The hallmark proliferating objects are corpses, victims of a plague and the hideous egocentricity it generates. In horrifyingly rapid succession, the characters fall victim not only to the disease but to suicide, murder, infanticide, cannibalism, and, finally, a raging fire. The only recurrent role in *The Killing Game* is that of a silent, hooded, black-robed monk, invisible to the other characters, whose appearance in each vignette foretells the next death. Since there are no other principal characters and no sustained plot, the actors are able to appear, die, reappear, and die again in any number of different configurations. (Ionesco suggests the use of puppets and dummies for crowd scenes.)

Among the most effective evocations of the infernal situation is a night scene combining an Artaudian barbarism with a Marx brothers–style bedlam. The shadows and sounds of threats, insults, theft, strangling, and murder are projected through lighted windows. In general, however, *The Killing Game* seems so closely modeled after Artaud's notion of the theater as plague that it verges on unintentional parody. The mechanical regularity with which the characters fall to horrible deaths ultimately becomes more sickly comic than tragic.

Macbett, which opened two years later, was written "to show one more time that every politician is paranoid and that all politics lead to crime" (*VR,* 162). Staring at his bloody sword, Macbett counts the dead from his recent battle. The number explodes from a first thought of "twelve dozen officers and men who never did me any harm" to a list of tens of millions dead from related causes. After a long soliloquy on man's appetite for carnage that conjures up Monty Pythonesque images of amputated arms still brandishing swords and pistols and legless feet that "kick us up the backside," Macbett fervently hopes that he hasn't trod on the toes of any friends and admits to feeling "a little queasy."[29] The effect of endless, mindless chaos and brutality is doubled when Banco, whose appearance and dress are so much like Macbett's that the two are frequently confused, immediately takes Macbett's place on stage and repeats his soliloquy word for word. In this harsh Jarryesque rewrite of Shakespeare's tragedy, Ionesco recovers the satiric verve of his early plays, though not their originality.

By the early 1970s, troubled by "murders, genocides, wars, Vietnam, Libya . . . the upheaval of societies," Ionesco found that the comic perspective of his absurd theater was no longer possible: "I put myself at a distance and I watch people, and everything they do seems, astonishing, ridiculous, insane . . . but no longer comic" (*VR,* 167). It was in this frame of mind that he wrote *Ce formidable bordel* (*What a Hell of a Mess*), which, like *Macbett,* attacks demagoguery and mindless carnage. The bored, uncommunicative protagonist, designated only as "the Character," is briefly jolted out of his antisocial existence when the customers at his habitual restaurant are transformed into Guignolesque revolutionaries preparing for an orgy of street violence with an impudent joie de vivre. At the end of the play, standing alone on a stage that has been emptied of props and decor as it was in *The Killer,* he bursts into laughter, having understood at last that life is a "a huge, overdone gag! And I worried and suffered."[30] This is not a particularly successful play. The Character is so clearly a foil for Ionesco that his despair is more tedious than convincing. On the whole, the apocalyptic plays are unwieldy mixtures of didacticism and surrealism.

Dream Theater: *L'Homme aux Valises (The Man with the Luggage)* and *Voyage chez les morts (Journeys among the Dead)*

Regarding his plays of the late 1960s, Ionesco blamed their oratorical quality and mixture of politics and personal material for their relative lack of success: "The fundamental error I made was that instead of telling about things that don't exist, I began to talk about myself and to defend particular points of view or ideas."[31] His next play, however, *The Man with the*

Luggage, written two years after *What a Hell of a Mess,* was a remarkably effective mix of politics and dreams. It is frankly autobiographical and oedipal. Ionesco described it as "my adolescence, even my childhood," animated by "the search for my own identity" (*VR,* 169). Its main character, First Man, is initially perceived on a dimly lit stage carrying two suitcases, whose contents are later revealed to include disguises, concrete mix, dolls, and vegetables. He claims to be missing a third one. The suitcases, according to Ionesco, represent the unconscious. Pursuing an identity in a country where he apparently was born but whose language he has forgotten, First Man struggles to come to terms with the dead but insufficiently buried past. His adventures center on a search for mother in an atmosphere heavy with Freudian and archetypal symbols and blackly humorous confrontations with father figures.

There is no cast of characters, only First Man has a fixed role. As in a dream, the other characters undergo metamorphoses not only from scene to scene but frequently from moment to moment. In the space of a nine-line conversation with First Man, a young woman ages by eight years. A Consul-Doctor-Tiresias figure turns into a psychiatrist; a sheriff is addressed as colonel and then becomes a judge; a tour guide turns into a policeman. Many of these metamorphic shifts are achieved with comic gags adopted from music hall routines and silent movies. Ionesco's political concerns, ranging from euthanasia to totalitarian governments, are woven into First Man's repeated, ineffective attempts to stand up to the abundant, unsympathetic father figures. In these encounters Ionesco captures the same terrifying vulnerability and bewildering isolation of the outsider that haunted Bérenger in *Rhinoceros.* The layering of personal and political concerns in the dreamlike folds of an age-old saga charges them with a universal anguish and significance. In the less successful *Journeys among the Dead* (1981), however, attempting to transfer essentially the same intimate dream material to the stage without any literary distortion, Ionesco fell into a trap he had warned others about many years earlier: "A playwright who is too conscious of what he is doing . . . winds up creating a work that is closed on itself."[32]

Ionesco was among the first to merge Dada's dismissal of reason, the surrealists' reach for another language and another dimension of reality in dreams, and existential pain into the rich dramatic resources of the theater of the absurd. The seductive quality of his most successful theater comes from an intensely visual imagination stirred by an acute awareness of the inadequacy of words to render the difficulty of being. "How," he once asked, "with the aid of words, can I express everything that words hide?" (*PP,* 168). He answered that question by framing his anguish in words and situations that were as wildly comical in their exaggeration as they were tragic in their consequences, and by creating a theater where violent physical effects and oneiric imagery compensate for the limited power of spoken language. Ionesco's theater is an extraordinary illustration of Artaud's contention that "to change the role of speech in theater is to make use of it in a concrete and spatial sense" (*TD,* 72).

Chapter Five

Arthur Adamov

"It is a fact: the young French theater is named Beckett, Adamov, Ionesco." That claim was made in 1956 on the front page of *Le Figaro* by Jean Anouilh, at the time France's best-known playwright. Adamov, who turned to the theater "to show on stage, as coarsely and as visibly as possible, human solitude, the absence of communication," was actually the first of the three to win recognition.[1] In 1950, when his still unperformed *La Parodie* (*The Parody*) and *L'Invasion* (*The Invasion*) were first published, they were prefaced by a flattering letter from André Gide and laudatory essays by several prominent literary and theater figures. Among those championing Adamov's cause was the young director Roger Blin, whose description of Adamov's "lucid buffoonery, despair . . . irremissible separation . . . obstinate tenderness," and "perpetually open trial of the absurd world" captured essential traits of the theater that would be later be christened the theater of the absurd (*IM,* 13). These enthusiastic endorsements held out a promise of recognition that remained largely unfulfilled. Adamov's absurd theater was eclipsed by that of Beckett and Ionesco. It was only when he turned to political theater in the mid-1950s that he achieved some measure of box office success.

Adamov's relative obscurity can be explained to a great extent by the blackness of his vision. His theater is rarely relieved by the fantasy that lightens Ionesco's or the lyricism and vaudeville humor that make Beckett's equally pessimistic assessment of human existence more palatable to audiences. Comedy is an important element in Adamov's plays, but what Blin referred to as his "lucid buffoonery" is also what in French is called *comédie grinçante,* comedy that makes the teeth grind. Adamov's theater has more in common with the harshness of German expressionism than the verbal antics of Dada and surrealism. His plays are also difficult to stage. Blin, who played the principal role in the first of Adamov's plays to reach the stage, *La Grande et la petite manoeuvre* (*The Great and the Small Maneuver*), blamed its lack of success on the difficulty of finding the right combination of realism and oneiric ambiguity.[2] The problem of style continued to plague productions of Adamov's theater, compounded by the limited means available to create sets that would convey the nightmarish atmosphere in which his early plays are meant to unfold. Adamov's plays also read somewhat roughly because they are heavily laced with indications for visual effects.

Adamov's theater is more uncomfortably autobiographical than Ionesco's or Beckett's, reflecting personal anguish and neuroses in a rawer form. It was not until the decades after his death, in 1970, when personal expression in the theater came to be valued over textual perfection, that the rougher but more human quality of his theater was appreciated. In a preface written in 1986 Ionesco reflected this evolution in attitude when he compared Adamov's theater to Beckett's, finding it "more human, more susceptible, clumsier, more destitute," but also more moving than "the perfect art, the hard but pitiless lucidity" of Beckett.[3] Adamov was a gifted playwright. His experiments with the physical language of the stage and his darkly comic treatment of isolation, helplessness, debilitation, and death deserved and still deserve far more recognition than has been their due. Three of his early plays in particular, *The Parody, The Great and the Small Maneuver,* and, especially, *Professor Taranne,* stand out as highly original examples of the theater of the absurd.

Background

Adamov was the quintessential exile among the absurdist playwrights. He was born in Russia on 23 August 1908 to an Armenian family possessing extensive oil fields on the Caspian Sea. The childhood he chronicles in his autobiographical essays, and reproduces in the nightmarish situations of his early theater, was made terrifying by the guilt and anxiety imposed by threatening parents and a cruelly teasing sister, and by the recurring violence of the Kurds against the Armenians. Ethnic tension prompted a family exodus to Germany in June 1914. Two months later the outbreak of World War I forced them into an eight-year exile in Geneva, a city Adamov was to remember for its audacious xenophobia.[4] In 1922, impoverished by the Bolsheviks' nationalization of the family's oil wells and by his father's obsessive gambling, Adamov's family returned to Germany. Adamov was introduced to German expressionism, whose harshly erotic and tortured subjects and antipathy to psychological theater heavily influenced his approach to the stage. Two years later the Adamovs moved to the suburbs of Paris. Although, as was usual for wealthy Russian children at the time, Adamov had been educated in French and considered it his native tongue, in Paris he remained a "displaced person" both emotionally and physically. Adamov frequented the cafés of Montparnasse, where he became friends with Artaud and Blin. For a while Adamov, who read Breton's *The Surrealist Revolution* with enthusiasm and wrote surrealist poetry, was accepted at the surrealists' gatherings. When he admitted preferring Baudelaire to Lautréamont and that his favorite contemporary poets were Paul Eluard and Tristan Tzara, however, he failed what he called Breton's "test for the little surrealist" and was excluded from the group.

Adamov's life during the years before World War II was tumultuous and painful. A disastrous love affair in 1928 prompted a nearly fatal suicide gesture, one that is repeated in several of his plays. His father committed suicide in 1933 in a room adjoining the one in which he was sleeping, exacerbating his already overwhelming anger and guilt: "I hated my father, therefore I killed him" (*HE,* 45). The temptation to take his own life hounded Adamov: "I wanted to commit suicide at age twenty, at age thirty, and again before I was forty" (*HE,* 14). In 1941 he was accused of hostility to the Vichy government and interned in a concentration camp for six months. He refused to join the Resistance movement in spite of the humiliation, something for which he later acknowledged feeling shame.

In 1946 Adamov published *L'Aveu* (The confession), a collection of self-revelatory texts. He had been working on *L'Aveu* since 1938, the same year he began translating Jung's *The Relations between the Ego and the Unconscious* and discovered Kafka, whose influence would later be very apparent in his theater. Encouraged by the success of *L'Aveu,* Adamov began to write seriously for the theater. The masochistic characters and humiliating situations in his early plays correspond very closely to the graphic descriptions in *L'Aveu* of his neuroses, impotence, and masochistic obsessions, and of the rituals he devised to dispel his obsessive fears. He became a prolific playwright. By the time of his death, in 1970, he had written 20 plays. He had also published autobiographical essays, a study of August Strindberg, and translations of major works by Georg Büchner, Heinrich von Kleist, August Strindberg, Gogol, Chekhov, Gorky, Erwin Piscator, Dostoyevski, and Max Frisch.

From *The Parody* to his transitional *Ping-Pong,* completed in 1955, Adamov's plays constituted an integral part of the theater of the absurd. In the mid-1950s, discouraged by the reception of his early plays and heavily influenced by Bertolt Brecht's theater, he turned to political and historical themes. Toward the end of his life he entered a third stage of his dramatic career, returning to the kind of parodical situations and experimentation with dream material that he had temporarily rejected as "grotesque and terrible."

The Absurdist Period: *From The Parody to Ping-Pong*

When Adamov began his career as a playwright, it was Artaud who represented for him "the truth of the theater" (*IM,* 84). Even when he later rejected the theater of the absurd, he continued to draw inspiration from Artaud: "When Antonin Artaud, in the middle of a poem, suddenly has an old woman say: 'how difficult, very difficult!' attempting thus to express very simply, very 'stupidly' the *real* difficulty of life, I find that much more true, much more tragic than when one speaks of the *absurdity* of life" (*IM,* 131–32). Like Artaud, Adamov was preoccupied with the debasement of language and attempted to renew the language of theater by emphasizing the physicality of the stage: "The theater as I conceive it is bound entirely and absolutely to representation" (*IM,* 13). Adamov's, like Artaud's, is a cruel theater, making extensive use of the Artaudian concept of the double.

Adamov's conviction that "a play ought to be the place where the visible world and the invisible world touch and collide with one another," also reflects a debt to Strindberg, the Swedish playwright acclaimed by the German expressionists as one of their masters (*IM,* 14). Adamov credited Artaud's 1927 production of Strindberg's *A Dream Play* with steering him to write for the theater. "What does Strindberg want essentially," Adamov asked, finding the answer to the question in the mirror of his own psyche: "to affirm, exhibit, prove and hide himself all at once. Where could he better satisfy these desires than on stage."[5] Inspired by what he described as "the appearance of a new time on the stage, a shorter time, the time of a dream" and the "visible changes of decor which are at the same time instantaneous changes of interior states" (*S,* 61–62), in Strindberg's theater, Adamov experimented with oneirically condensed time and fluid stage imagery.

La Parodie (The Parody) Adamov often recounted the incident that was the source of his first play: "A blind man was begging. Two young girls pass without seeing him, bump into him inadvertently; they were singing: 'I closed my eyes, it was wonderful'" (*IM,* 17). The characters in *The Parody,* which begins with the sounds of an offstage eye examination, can neither "see" nor "hear" one another. Blindly narcissistic, they create such different languages from the same words that each becomes deaf to the others' meaning. Their dialogue becomes a parody of communication.

The Parody juxtaposes four nameless male characters—N., the Employee, the Journalist, and the Director—and a female character, almost as impersonally named Lily.[6] Each of the men wants Lily. Both N. and the

Employee are wrongly persuaded that Lily has promised a rendezvous and waste away in a grimly comical pursuit. "I started from a general idea . . . all destinies are equivalent, the refusal of life (N.) and its complacent acceptance (the Employee) both end in inevitable failure, in total destruction" (*IM,* 18). The Employee, who is initially as obtusely optimistic and agitated as N. is pessimistic and lethargic, winds up a literally blind, broken prisoner of an unseen but noisily omnipresent police force. N., very clearly a shadow of his creator, spends much of the time lying about in the street. In his first encounter with Lily, he begs her to kill him since he is already dead: "Everybody is dead, not only me. Look at them blink their eyes, as if they were always getting cold rain in the face. They pretend to be walking, and at each step it is like two brooms balancing to the left and right."[7] N.'s death finally comes in a manner reminiscent of Adamov's suicidal gesture in 1928. He is run over by a car. When the curtain comes up on the last tableau, N.'s bloody body is lying onstage, arms stretched out in a cross. Lily doesn't see it and bumps into it. Two sanitation workers appear and matter-of-factly sweep N. from the stage like ordinary trash. The brightest light of the play is reserved for this brutal moment, illuminating the emptiness of human existence. The stage directions indicate that the moment the broom touches N., the lighting is to become as harsh and bright as possible and a background is to appear that seems as real as possible and "perfectly empty, raw and cold."

Martin Esslin notes that the original meaning of the word *absurd* is "out of harmony" (Esslin, 23). All the elements of *The Parody,* linguistic and physical, are out of harmony. Set against a blurry, circular black-and-white photograph at the back of the stage and accompanied by the discordant sounds of impersonal city life, voices, police sirens, and typewriters, the action unfolds in rushed, jerky, dreamlike sequences of puppetlike agitation and missed cues. A municipal clock without hands, which grows bigger from one part to the next, stands at the side of the stage. Characters constantly ask each other for the time but receive either no answer or a brusque command to look at the clock. Time in this parody of human expectations is measured by abrupt physical decay and by the shrinking of hopes, a phenomenon that Adamov renders concretely by shrinking the stage sets from part 1 to part 2, in contrast to the "growing" clock. The characters visibly decay, succumbing to disabilities and a telescopic aging process. Only the Director, who plays three different roles and is a prototype of the unsavory capitalist chameleons in Adamov's theater, resists the progressive collapse. N.'s degradation represents most graphically the paralyzing absurdity of human existence. He regresses from exhausted stumbling to complete immobility before being impersonally crushed to death. His fate is foreshadowed in an earlier scene, in which the Director becomes so busy signing his name that he drowns the immobile N. in the papers that are spilling from his desk onto the office floor.

Roger Blin directed the premiere of *The Parody* in June 1952 in the small theater where Ionesco's *The Chairs* had opened just six weeks before. It folded quickly, drawing only about 15 people a night. One of the prefatory essays to the 1950 edition had predicted that "when *The Parody,* where the figures of desire and anguish led by time destroy themselves in their journey toward an unattainable escape, finds a place on stage, then it will be understood that a profoundly modern theater . . . is affirming and explaining itself."[8] This did not turn out to be the case in 1952. "Adamov," according to a reviewer for *Le Figaro,* "is one of these painters who paint boredom with boredom. . . . he creates absurd theater by placing shorthand sentences end to end. There is, on the whole, in this spectacle a taste for the infamous, a pleasure in vileness that is rightly unbearable" (Latour, 262).

La Grande et la petite manoeuvre (The Great and the Small Maneuver) *The Great and the Small Maneuver* (1950) is perhaps the best illustration of the goal Adamov set for himself in his early plays: to make the staging "coincide literally, *concretely, corporally*" with the contents of the play (*IM,* 14). Like *The Parody,* it involves a passive victim, the Mutilé, and an activist, the Militant. In this Kafkaesque play both are maneuvered to failure, victims of their own psyches (the "great maneuver") and politics (the "small maneuver").[9] Adamov chose the title because, he claimed, "it is more correct to say of threatened man that he is in reality *maneuvered:* each of my characters is persecuted but without being able to say from what side the persecution comes. It comes from everywhere and men *maneuver* all along fear" (Latour, 59).

The source of *Maneuver* was a terrifying dream in which Adamov was summoned to self-destructive activities by voices from loudspeakers. The phantasmagoric effect is recaptured in the play in the rapidity and abruptness with which the 10 short tableaux follow one another, and in the nightmarish grip created by the staging, which from the opening moments of the first tableau establishes a context of blind manipulation and brutality. The curtain rises on a dark, empty stage. Cold, even voices from the loudspeakers issue orders to an unidentified victim. From offstage comes a noise of clapping hands, a sound whose savage irony is later revealed when the Mutilé begins to lose his limbs. As the lights come up, the Militant is brought onstage and roughed up by two policemen. In tandem with the physical battering taking place on stage, Adamov continues to assault the audience acoustically with the monitors' voices, the clapping, and the sound of hostile laughter coming from the wings.

In dreamlike shifts of time and place, the subsequent tableaux, which Adamov conceived as having "an almost cinematic linking," present the destruction of the Mutilé and his brother-in-law, the Militant, a member of a revolutionary group called the Partisans. The Militant, whose blind adherence to the demands of the revolutionary movement causes the death of his son and ruins his marriage, is essentially destroyed by his own rhetoric. Articulating the eternal untruths of demagogues, the victorious Partisans adopt the same power-hungry behavior as that of the reactionary government they replaced. Adamov's recurring theme of the degeneration of language is broadened in *Maneuver* to encompass linguistic manipulation for political ends. In a parallel but more graphically horrifying phenomenon, the Mutilé is progressively dismembered in response to mysterious orders from monitors, which no one else hears. Adamov, as cruelly as Beckett, uses physical degradation to portray the debilitating effect of modern society. As soon as the Mutilé hears the monitors' voices, he begins to shake. After minimal resistance, he simply crosses his arms, an action that becomes particularly grotesque when they have been reduced to stumps, and slinks away to submit. The inadmissibly brutal mutilation becomes a source of cruel humor, both when the Mutilé attempts to cross his ineffective stumps and when he enrolls in a typing course for the disabled. As the typing students struggle, the director and her assistant engage in constant hand play and make tactless references to hands. Laughing, however uncomfortably, at the inappropriate words and gestures, the spectator or reader is forced to acknowledge an unwitting alliance with the persecuting "others" in the play. This is precisely the kind of cruel theater promoted by Artaud.

The first of Adamov's plays to be performed, *Maneuver* received mixed reviews and had only 25 performances. Camus congratulated Adamov for *Maneuver*, but Adamov's approach in this play was deliberately anti-Sartrean and anti-Camusian. Defending his theater, which he expected to be judged "puerile" in contrast to the philosophical theater then in vogue, Adamov maintained, "If the drama of a man consists in any kind of a mutilation of his person, I do not see a better means to render the truth of such a mutilation dramatically than to represent it physically on stage . . . for me it is precisely in this puerility that all the resources of a living theater reside" (*IM*, 22).

Le Professeur Taranne (Professor Taranne) Adamov created the two short tableaux of *Professor Taranne* very rapidly in 1951 from another dream. In *Taranne,* according to Adamov, for the first time he was able simply to transcribe a dream without distorting it for ulterior motives. The naturalness with which he captures a dream's fluid time and settings and its capacity to condense complex webs of fear and desire into a few indelible images makes *Taranne* an exceptional play. He described Taranne as "a premonitory text. My fear of being nothing but a lecturer, a traveling salesman, the author invited abroad, ignored in France" (*HE,* 101).

The play opens with the professor in a police station, defending himself in an ineffective rush of words against the charge of appearing naked on the beach. He bases his defense on the fact that he is Professor Taranne, known by everyone. No one in the police station has heard of him, however. The one person who thinks she recognizes Taranne mistakes him for a Professor Menard. A journalist familiar with the university not only claims not to know Taranne but essentially denies his existence by turning away from him when he tries to introduce himself. Abandoned in the police station, Taranne rushes off, frantic because he hasn't signed the necessary papers. His terrified voice can be heard from the wings: "I don't understand."[10] Taranne joins the many Adamovian characters for whom imposing one's existence, even just enough to be recognized as physically present, is an insurmountable obstacle.

A dreamlike shift, brought about by the appearance of a hotel manageress who slightly adjusts the furniture and hangs a rack of keys on the wall, transforms the police station into the reception area of Taranne's hotel. His key is missing. Two policemen enter looking for Taranne, now accused of strewing papers in beach cabins. Taranne undertakes another rambling, implausible defense, in which his identity becomes even more questionable. While Taranne loses himself in unlikely excuses, the policemen slip offstage. The hotel manageress returns and hands Taranne an enormous roll of paper. Spreading it out in the middle of the stage, Taranne reveals a dining room seating plan for a steamship on which he had failed to book passage. He has been assigned a place at the head table. Taranne's sister appears and reads a letter from the rector at the university where Taranne claims to be so highly regarded denouncing his incompetence and accusing him of plagiarizing a Professor Menard and even stealing his eyeglasses. Literally staggering from the blow, Taranne grasps at the table to keep from falling as he asks: "Why tell me this now, after all these years? Why hasn't he told me sooner? Why haven't they all told me?

Because it's obvious! You can see it immediately!" (*TP,* 29). But Taranne, although accused in the first act of watching all the time and seeing too much, inhabits, like the other characters in Adamov's early plays, a world in which people cannot or will not see.

The sister disappears. The hotel manager comes in and, without looking at Taranne, empties the stage of all its properties except for an incriminating notebook, the letter, and the seating plan. Taranne doesn't notice. He tacks the seating plan to the wall, revealing only a large empty surface. Taranne has no visible place, not even on paper. With his back turned to the audience, he stares at the blank plan for a long moment and then very slowly begins to undress as the curtain falls. It is an ambiguous ending typical of the theater of the absurd. Taranne is the kind of alienated individual for whom the terms *guilty* or *innocent* make no sense, since he has been allotted no place among the smug ranks of people sure enough of their own roles to be willing to make that kind of judgment.

In *Professor Taranne* Adamov achieved an effect he had admired much earlier in a scene in Strindberg's *The Road to Damascus:* "To translate the painful impression . . . of a rapid transformation and degradation of places and beings, impression of half-sleep but also the reality of fear and discouragement" (*AS,* 61). As in a dream, it is primarily the physical language that tells the story, usually in contradiction to Taranne's words. Taranne is unable to defend himself against the solid, accusatory muteness of the stage properties. Stripped of his words, the doubly naked, ridiculous, and probably dishonest Taranne becomes one of the most unforgettable Nobody-as-Everyman figures to appear on the twentieth-century stage. With *Taranne,* Adamov had accomplished what he once claimed was the only task left: "to tear away all the dead skin, to strip oneself to the point of finding oneself at the hour of the great nakedness."[11] Unfortunately, Adamov had no more luck with his *Taranne* in Paris, where it opened in May 1954, than with his previous plays, although by then the theater of the absurd was becoming a more familiar phenomenon.

Transition: *Le Ping-Pong (Ping-Pong)* Increasingly frustrated by the contrast between the growing success of Beckett and Ionesco and his own continued condemnation to offnight performances, Adamov began to chafe at the limits of his absurdist theater. In *Ping-Pong,* completed in 1955, he made a transition to a more politicized theater by introducing multidimensional characters who are crushed not by a vague but inexorable fate but by a fixation on pinball machines and a desire to "make it" that drops them in the maw of a capitalist corporation. Adamov conceived the title image—"two old men . . . whose deplorable habit of complicating everything pushes them to complicate even the game of Ping-Pong" (Latour, 68–69)—before he knew what he would make of it in the play. Instead of Ping-Pong, pinball became the controlling image: "I wanted everything in the play to revolve around the pinball machine . . . every worry, every nostalgia, every ambition" (*HE,* 112). Each of the characters sacrifices whatever limited financial or creative resources he or she possesses to a consortium that controls the economics of the pinball industry. The destructively mesmerizing behavior of the unreliable pinball machines and the consortium that controls them is mirrored in the progressively dehumanized mechanical relationships of the characters. In the last scene of the play, the main characters, Arthur and Victor, who were young at the beginning of the play, are white-haired old men. Still quarrelling over points and procedures as they used to during the pinball games in their youth, they play the Ping-Pong match that gives the play its title. The game grows progressively madder as they invent new rules. The net is thrown away, then the paddles. Shouting in anger, they leap about, using their hands as paddles, until Victor suddenly falls dead. The comically degenerate but tragically lethal Ping-Pong game is Adamov's mirror image of a society in which scheming has replaced intelligence, and addiction and rapaciousness have replaced desire.

Ping-Pong, which Adamov considered the most comic of his plays—"comedy a little grinding, no doubt, but a deliberate turning of the back to the falsely tragic expressionism of my first plays" (Latour, 68)—is tied to the theater of the absurd by the treatment of language. In the sometimes humorous, sometimes irritating, stilted, and inflated dialogues, words become the empty, addictive equivalent of a pinball game. The lines addressed to a snoring old woman by a down-and-out former employee of the consortium reflects a world held captive by the machinery of its language: "Yes," he exclaims, walking about like a madman and knocking a dead body that has been laid out on chairs to the floor, "the sleeping traveler inside me awakened and called and I answered, 'Here!' Import-export, U.S.A. How does that sound to you? . . . In the States they have big ideas. They see things on a big scale. Ideas have consequences, people take action, the bidding rises, people put money on you, double or nothing, the winner and still champ, drive, it's all drive. Once you've got drive, the machine runs itself and it runs and runs."[12]

The most successful of Adamov's plays to date, *Ping-Pong* was still not the theatrical victory Adamov dreamed of nor the financial success he so desperately needed. After *Ping-Pong* he severed his ties with the theater of the absurd for several years. "Little by little, writing *Ping-Pong,* I began to judge my first plays severely and, very sincerely, criticized *Waiting for Godot* and *The Chairs* for the same reasons. I already saw in the 'avant-garde' an easy escape, a diversion from real problems. . . . Life wasn't absurd, but difficult, very difficult" (*HE,* 111).

Brechtian Theater

Adamov's discouragement with his absurdist theater coincided with an increasingly indignant awareness of the politics of the Fifth Republic and his discovery of Brecht, who replaced Strindberg, Artaud, and Kafka as the dominant influences on his theater. *Paolo Paoli,* the first of Adamov's Brechtian plays, satirizes the speculative greed of pre–World War I society. Brecht's influence is evident in *Paolo Paoli* in both the often humorous treatment of the political topic and in the distancing effect of the staging, which calls for the breaking up of the tableaux by projections of historical photographs and newspaper excerpts from the days just before World War I. *Paolo Paoli* was followed by *Le Printemps '71* (Spring '71), a massive historical epic depicting the insurrection and brutal repression of the Paris Communards in 1871. Adamov's debt to Brecht, who had written a play on the same topic, is again evident in the alienating device of allegorical "Guignol" interludes, where real actors, not puppets, adopt exaggeratedly repellent styles to portray repressive historical figures or institutions. Made up of 26 scenes, interspersed with nine allegorical "Guignols," and an epilogue, it is a forerunner of the vast spectacles that came into vogue in the French theater in the 1970s.

La Politique des restes (*The Politics of Waste*), completed in 1962, is set in South Africa but was inspired by Adamov's discovery of Harlem during a trip to New York City. In the 1967 Paris production, images of poor black neighborhoods in American cities and slums in the Paris environs were projected between the scenes.[13] Adamov made two trips to the United States, the first in 1959 for a disastrous New York production of *Ping-Pong,* the second when he was invited to be a visiting lecturer at Cornell University in the fall of 1964. In 1968 he wrote *Off Limits,* another harshly anti-American play. Using a party given by a wealthy New Yorker as his framework, he breaks the episodes into a series of happenings, allowing him to take on both the politics of the Vietnam War era and the society responsible for a generation lost to drugs.

The Absurd Renewed

Although the years that correspond to Adamov's political theater continued to be difficult, this period was the most successful of his career. His left-leaning theater brought new audiences, more sympathetic than Left Bank audiences had been to his absurdist plays. Several of his plays were performed outside of France. Toward the end of his career, however, still discouraged by the reception of his plays in France, and suffering the effects of years of alcohol and drug addiction, Adamov renewed some of his ties to the theater of the absurd: "I wanted to go back to my former 'absurd' theater. . . . But I believe that in these last plays I have united, reunited, a little better than in the past individual psychology and the general political line" (*Théâtre,* 3:9). With the exception of his last play, *Si l'été revenait* (*If Summer Were to Return*), none of these plays is as powerful as his early works, nor were they particularly successful.

The ironically named *Sainte Europe* (*Holy Europe*), completed in 1966, is a burlesque epic in which actors alternate between allegorical dreams and realistic waking scenes, playing caricatural dual roles as medieval figures and modern political dignitaries. In *M. le Modéré* (*Mr. Moderate,* 1967) which Adamov called a "clownerie," he again attacks the decadence of contemporary European politics, particularly the role of the moderates, and the intrusive role of American policy in European affairs, but scales the stature of the main characters and their political ambitions to *Ubu*esque dimensions. Through comically implausible circumstances involving an American agent, the narcissistic and excessively moderate M. le Modéré, a hotel keeper in Paris, becomes the chief officer of the Jura in Switzerland and is charged with putting down a rebellion. His devices for income-generating methods of punishment, although a little gentler than Ubu's, involve the same kind of pernicious, self-centered logic and bombastic rhetoric. He is exiled finally to London, where he is confined to a wheelchair by a stroke and becomes an alcoholic. This cruel play represented a moment of reckoning for Adamov, who was once more in the hospital suffering from drug and alcohol abuse when he wrote it: "Hemmed in by misery, I had to either burst out laughing or commit suicide" (*Théâtre,* 4:11). When it was staged in Paris in 1968, the director set the action in a hospital, putting M. le Modéré in pajamas for the entire play. The scenery was changed by nurses to the sound of ambulance sirens (Gaudy, 87).

If Summer Were to Return, a final, Strindbergian reworking of Adamov's neuroses and his failure as a playwright, is presented as a series of four dreams. The central figure, Lars, is a repressed and brutal son; a failure as a brother, husband, and friend; and a failure at any profession. Like his desperately ill creator, he wears pajamas during much of the play. Each of the four dream sequences alters the perspective on Lars. As one character dreams, the others stand to the side of the stage acting out the dream's hidden meaning. A seesaw onstage physically captures the ambivalence and instability of the characters' relationships. *If Summer Were to Return* was completed two and a half months before Adamov's death, in 1970, from an overdose of barbiturates.

Paying homage to Adamov's theater in 1976, Roger Planchon, a director who worked closely with Adamov for many years, described it as "fundamental for all those who are interested in the adventure of theater," and, although he worried that Adamov was in danger of becoming "an author for authors the way some poets exist only for other poets," he forecast that "future generations might one day be more drawn by the hesitations and imperfections in Adamov's theater than to the perfections of Beckett's."[14] There has been a renewed interest in the last decade in Adamov's experiments with stage language and their adaptability to both absurdist and political themes. In 1975 Planchon created a very successful spectacle entitled *A.A.: Théâtres d'Arthur Adamov,* a collage of episodes from his early plays and autobiographical writings. Consummate exhibitionist, masochist, and ironist that Adamov was, he might have found a perverse pleasure in the fact that Planchon had a greater box office success with his *A.A.* than Adamov had had with most of his own plays. "When I arrange the world around me," Adamov wrote, "I often reproach it for being nothing more than a parody."[15]

Chapter Six
Jean Genet

For Genet the theater was a mirror: "I go to the theater in order to see myself, on the stage . . . such as I wouldn't know how—or wouldn't dare—to see myself or to dream myself, and such, however, as I know myself to be."[1]

Sartre's comparison of Genet to Narcissus crystallizes the elaborate web of reflected images that constitutes Genet's theater: "Not all who would be are Narcissus. Many who lean over the water see only a vague human figure. Genet sees himself everywhere; the dullest surfaces reflect his image; even in others he perceives himself, thereby bringing to light their deepest secrets. The disturbing theme of the double, the image, the counterpart, the enemy brother, is found in all his works."[2]

Profoundly romantic, Genet also sought in theater the magic and mystery of a religious rite. He dreamed of a monumental eroticized theater that would "have as much importance as the Palace of Justice, the monument to the dead, the cathedral, the Chamber of Deputies, the War College, the seat of government, the Observatory," combining all those functions "as if in a cemetery, or next to a crematory with a stiff, oblique and phallic chimney" (*OC,* 4:14).

Genet's plays, with their dreamlike time, stylized language, powerful visual imagery, preoccupation with masks and doubles, and blasphemous, perverted rituals, inevitably invite comparison to Artaud's theater. The extent of Artaud's influence on Genet has been a subject of much debate, however. For Robert Brustein, persuaded that "Genet, the dramatist . . . is largely created by Artaud," the possibility that Artaud had not directly influenced Genet's theater would be "one of the most extraordinary coincidences in literary history."[3] Roger Blin, who worked more closely with Genet than any other director, doubted that Artaud's ideas influenced his work, although he suggested that they had affected his personality.[4] Whether or not there was direct influence, there is no question that their dramatic "missions" (the religious connotation of the word is applicable) were similar. Each converted private obsessions and a determinedly antisocial personal history into spectacular productions meant to threaten the moral, linguistic, and social foundations of the audience. "Evil," Genet wrote, "must explode on the stage, show us naked, leave us wild-eyed if possible and with no other recourse than ourselves" (*OC,* 4:35).

Background

Genet was born in Paris in 1910, an illegitimate child who became a ward of the state. At age seven he was placed with a peasant couple as a foster child. In the rural milieu, where roots in the land were the anchoring element of one's identity, he was cruelly ostracized by his schoolmates. According to the legend fostered by Sartre, and later by Genet as well, it was this kind of early experience that turned Genet into an outlaw. Genet began to steal at a young age. Branded a thief, he became a determined one. When he was 15, he was sent to the reform school at Mettray, where he stayed for three years. At Mettray, a hierarchical milieu fostering criminal attitudes and betrayal, he discovered that he could forge an admired identity as a tough homosexual delinquent. After Mettray, Genet joined and then deserted the Foreign Legion. From 1930 to 1942 he wandered in the criminal underworld of Europe and North Africa. It was a vagabondage of begging, theft, smuggling, pimping, and prostitution that took him from prison to prison and provided the settings and character models for his novels and first play. Genet began writing in prison. His first novel, *Our Lady of the Flowers* (1944), was begun on the brown paper distributed to the prisoners for making bags. Genet's writing was discovered and promoted by Jean Cocteau, then by Sartre, whose *Saint Genet: Comedian and Martyr,* a massive biography and existentialist psychoanalysis of Genet's early work, made him into an almost mythical figure. In 1948, fearing that Genet would be condemned to life imprisonment as a habitual criminal, Cocteau, Sartre, Breton, and a number of other well-known writers successfully appealed for a presidential pardon. By 1948 Genet had published his autobiographical *Thief's Journal* and four novels and had completed two plays, the second of which, *The Maids,* had been successfully performed in Paris in 1947.

Haute Surveillance (Deathwatch)

Genet's first play is set in a prison cell. The title comes from a French prison term for the close watch that is kept over a prisoner awaiting execution. In this tight setting, reminiscent of Sartre's *Huis clos,* three prisoners—Green Eyes, a murderer; LeFranc, a petty thief; and Maurice, an effeminate juvenile delinquent—confront each other in a struggle to impose fantasized identities. Green Eyes is the "god" of the cell, but only a demigod in the larger context of the prison, which is dominated by a black murderer named Snowball. Snowball never appears, but his offstage presence shapes and eventually destroys the Green Eyes/LeFranc/Maurice triangle. LeFranc, jealous of Green Eyes' criminal status and Maurice's sexual intimacy with him, attempts to alienate Maurice's affection by comparing his hero and lover unfavorably to Snowball.

Green Eye's opening lines warn LeFranc: "Stop the big act, and stop talking about the Negro."[5] In Genet's dramatic world, however, playacting, which becomes a kind of existential thievery, is a necessary defense. Maurice has filched a prison identity by grafting himself onto Green Eyes's aura. Puffed up with this illusory identification, he enrages LeFranc, taunting him with his inked-on tatoo and stolen facade: "You dress yourself up, you decorate yourself with our jewels, I accuse you! You steal our crimes!" (*MD,* 158). LeFranc strangles Maurice while Green Eyes watches with disgusted indifference from an elevated position on an overturned washbasin. With this crime, LeFranc aspires to become one with Green Eyes and to take his "luminous place." Green Eyes belittles the murder because it was willed and not, as his murder was, a gratuitous gift "from god or the devil, but something I didn't want" (*MD,* 160). Although not destined for the ranks of the prison elect, LeFranc transforms his defeat and solitude into an existentialist apotheosis: "I won't have to dance to undo my crime, because I willed it" (*MD,* 161).[6]

Deathwatch, which is the least performed of Genet's plays, is a powerful early example of his violently physical stage language. The brief stage directions emphasize a ritualistic delivery and an oneiric theatricality. They call for a harshly lit stage with set and costumes colored in "hard blacks" clashing against white. The actors' movements are to be "either heavy or else extremely and incomprehensibly rapid," the timbre of their voices deadened (*MD,* 103–4). The dialogue in *Deathwatch* functions like a stylized theatrical mask. Combining argot and an exalted formal lyricism, Genet turns speech into something fraudulent. Like LeFranc's inked-on tattoo, language is "something from a book."

Deathwatch was first performed in Paris in 1949, directed by Louis Jouvet, who had staged *The Maids* two years earlier. Critical reaction, as much a response to Genet's personal life as to his theater, was generally negative. Jean-Jacques Gauthier's dismissal was predictably vitriolic: "We have had our bellyful of these nauseous exhalations from the kitchen sink, of these self-satisfied stinks from intellectual latrines."[7]

Les Bonnes (The Maids)

The Maids, another one-act play, is similar in many ways to *Deathwatch.* In both plays, a single, confined, eroticized setting (a bedroom in *The Maids*) alternately suffocates and exalts a trio of characters, and in both a triangular configuration is destroyed by an absent, dominating male. In *The Maids,* as in *Deathwatch,* but more powerfully, the magic of language and ritual transform erotic fantasies into a deadly image.

In the opening scene, a maid called Claire prepares her mistress to go out for the evening. The mistress is verbally abusive; the maid is both exaggeratedly subservient and insolent. As the audience struggles to find bearings in this situation, which is both realistic and strangely distorted, an alarm clock rings and shatters the illusion. The two women are not maid and mistress but sisters, both maids, enacting a daily ritual in which they take turns playing Madame and whichever maid the maid-playing sister is not. Claire is not Claire but Solange. Playing the role of Madame, she insults her own image. The ritual is supposed to culminate in a symbolic murder of Madame, but the alarm clock always rings too soon. As the maids attempt to restore order, terrified that the objects in the room will betray their game to the real Madame, they are interrupted by the telephone. Madame's lover, whom they had denounced to the police in anonymous letters, has called to announce his release from prison. Giddy with words of hate and desire, and illusions of salvation through crime, they decide to kill Madame by poisoning her tea before she discovers their betrayal. Madame returns. She is a performer, like her maids, and revels in preparations for the romantic role (already performed by the maids in their earlier ritual) of devotedly following her lover to a penal colony. When she inadvertently learns that her lover has been freed, Madame rushes off, refusing to drink the tea. Claire and Solange return to their ritual. Claire/Madame orders Solange/Claire to bring her the poisoned tea. At the end of the play, she drinks it.

The Maids is based on a real incident in 1933 involving two maids, the Papin sisters, whose highly sensationalized trial rallied the intellectual left to their cause. Genet, however, was adamant that his play was not a plea for social justice. His concern was to place this revelatory ritual before his terrible theatrical mirror: "Sacred or not, these maids are monsters, like ourselves when we dream this or that" (*OC,* 4:269). Genet wanted every element of the play to emphasize the theatricality of the maids' situation, calling for unrealistic costumes and gestures, and a highly stylized mixture of popular language and poetic transport: "Already disturbed by the dismal bleakness of a theatre that reflects the visible world too exactly, the actions of men and not of gods, I attempted to effect a displacement that, in permitting a declamatory tone, would bring theatre into the theatre."[8] The last lines of the play, recited by Solange, who faces the audience while Claire drinks the poisoned tea, remind the spectators that this is theater: "The orchestra is playing brilliantly. The attendant is raising the red velvet curtain" (*MD,* 99).

The maids' ceremony, hinging on words and images as chimerical as LeFranc's "Avenger" tatoo, ritualizes a volatile set of relationships. Conforming to a love-hate bond with their mistress, a compound of maternal affection and homosexual desire, it also highlights the sickening reflection of a hated self that vitiates the alliance between the two maids: "I'm sick of seeing my image thrown back at me by a mirror, like a bad smell. You're my bad smell" (*MD,* 61). Its primary dramatic function is to generate a linguistic model for an apotheosizing merger of identities through the suicide/murder. In order to persuade the frightened Solange to serve the poisoned tea, Claire feeds her words as though she were celebrating Mass. The words take on a magical power, temporarily masking the maids' intolerable, imposed condition with a willingly assumed image in which the two sisters become one: "Now we are Mademoiselle Solange Lemercier, that Lemercier woman. The famous criminal" (*MD,* 95). Solange's epilogue at the end of the play is a vision of the two maids rising up, "free, from Madame's icy form. . . . We are beautiful, joyous, drunk, and free!" (*MD,* 100). With the words that ritualize the maids' hatred and ennoble their crime, Genet too triumphs over the manners and myths of bourgeois society.

The Maids has been the most widely and frequently performed of Genet's plays. Even in 1947, Louis Jouvet's production had a run of some 80 performances. It has invited radical interpretations and staging. In 1963 Jean-Marie Serreau emphasized the theme of social rejection by casting two black actresses from the West Indies as Claire and Solange. There have been several productions with male actors playing all three roles, sparked by Genet's statement in *Our Lady of the Flowers* that if he were to have a play performed in which women had roles, he would have the parts played by adolescent boys. In 1969 Victor Garcia interpreted *The Maids* as a Black Mass.

Le Balcon (The Balcony)

Several years passed before another of Genet's plays was performed, a hiatus that he attributed to the stifling effect of Sartre's *Saint Genet.* When he returned with *The Balcony* in 1956, his fundamental themes were not much changed. The characters (and spectators) are again sucked into a vortex of eroticized illusions already familiar from *Deathwatch* and *The Maids.* Genet's dramatic vision, however, had become more elaborate and humorous. Most of the action in the nine tableaux of *The Balcony* (there were 15 in the original version) takes place in the flexible grandiosity of a brothel, a *maison d'illusions* (house of illusions), as it is known in French slang. The Grand Balcony is the creation of Madame Irma, who controls a dazzling range of studios by means of an elaborate set of mirrors, a kind of periscopic switchboard, and a comically unbending insistence on limiting her clients' fantasies to the paid-for time limit. The brothel setting, admiringly described by the Chief of Police as a "sumptuous theatre where every moment a drama is performed—in the sense that the outside world says a mass is celebrated,"[9] lends itself to spectacular treatment of the problem of image versus function at the heart of this play.

The Balcony begins like *The Maids* as theater within the theater, but unlike *The Maids,* in which the initial false maid/mistress scene appears very real, the first scene in *The Balcony* is stridently theatrical. The curtain goes up on a bishop in miter and gilded cope, ostentatiously pardoning a provocatively dressed young woman. Three blood-red folding screens form a violent backdrop. A huge Spanish cross drawn in trompe l'oeil hangs down. The bishop's stature is exaggerated by shoulder pads and cothurni, the high shoes worn by actors in ancient Greek and Roman tragedies, and both bishop and penitent are garishly made up. In a gilded mirror the image of an unmade bed is reflected at an angle that would require it to be placed in the first rows of the orchestra. The illusion is destroyed by Madame Irma, who interrupts the bishop's fantasies of cruel pardons and a sensual death in his episcopal finery with the reminder that his time is up. The bishop is a gas man and his lace-clad penitent one of Madame Irma's employees. In equally ornate settings, with the same mirror reflecting the unmade bed, similar scenes are played out in the next two tableaux. In the second scene, a larger-than-life judge confronts a bare-breasted thief. In the third, a general in full regalia, his prostitute serving as his mare, dreams of death "where I shall be nothing, though reflected *ad infinitum* in these mirrors, nothing but my image" (*B,* 26). For Genet, the brothel clients' sadomasochistic masquerades in the visual and verbal splendor of bishop, judge, and general are no more fraudulent than the "playing" of these roles by their real life counterparts. "In real life," Madame Irma points out, "they're props of a display that they have to drag in the mud of the real and commonplace. Here, Comedy and Appearance remain pure, and the Revels intact" (*B,* 36).

The revels of the brothel are periodically interrupted by the sounds of machine gun fire. Outside, an armed rebellion is taking place, aimed at the totalitarian order whose roles and stage effects have been enshrined in the Grand Balcony. In the fifth scene, which takes place in Madame Irma's office/bedroom, the outside world penetrates the sanctuary of the brothel with the arrival of the Chief of Police. He brings news of the battle, but his primary concern is whether one of Irma's customers has "consecrated" his image by asking to impersonate him. No one has. His image, which he conceives as a gigantic phallus, "a prick of great stature," to symbolize, he tells Irma, "the nation, your joint," does not yet conform to the "liturgies of the brothel" (*B,* 78).

The action moves briefly to the rebellion in the streets, the "real" world whose aims and props are exposed by Genet as mirror images of the illusions of the brothel. The rebel leader, a young plumber named Roger, has persuaded one of Madame Irma's employees to join him. He watches helplessly as the rebels transform her into the symbol of their revolt: "In order to fight against an image Chantal has frozen into an image. The fight is no longer taking place in reality, but in the lists. Field azure. It's the combat of allegories. None of us know any longer why we revolted" (*B,* 57). Recognizing that to save the old order requires only that its figureheads appear intact, the Chief of Police controls the scenarios of the revolt with the techniques of the brothel. In a parallel to the fourth scene, where a brothel client's desired image is "mirrored" for him by three actors playing the roles of the reflections, he persuades Irma to dress up as the queen and her clients to put on their brothel costumes and assume the symbolic functions of bishop, judge, and general. They appear on the balcony of the brothel to the cheers of the people below. The brothel bishop orders Chantal shot. The revolution is crushed.

The first client to appear at the reopened brothel is Roger. Impersonating the Chief of Police, Roger castrates himself. With this act of illusory identification and vengeance, he joins the self-destructive league of LeFranc in *Deathwatch* and the two sisters in *The Maids,* claiming "I've a right to lead the character I've chosen to the very limit of his destiny . . . no, of mine . . . of merging his destiny with mine" (*B,* 93). Overjoyed to at last "belong to the nomenclature," once he has assured himself that he is still intact, the Chief of Police retreats into a mausoleum resembling General Franco's where, Christ-like, "larger than large, stronger than strong, deader than dead," he will magnify his image for two thousand years (*B,* 94).[10] As the play ends, the revolt starts up again. Madame Irma turns to the spectators and tells them to go home, "where everything—you can be quite sure—will be falser than here" (*B,* 96).

Critics and scholars often treat *The Balcony* as a sociopolitical piece.[11] Directors, on the other hand, have tended to de-emphasize or eliminate altogether the revolutionary scenes, finding them clumsily integrated into the work as a whole and peripheral to the more central issue of appearances. Genet reduced the number of revolutionary scenes in the revised edition, although he had earlier expressed displeasure when Peter Brook cut from them in his Paris production. Nevertheless, the context of political revolt is fundamental to the meaning of *The Balcony.* Genet's assumption that revolutionary movements are corrupted by the power of their symbols in the very process of coming into being, and that the conflicts and trappings of power are a sexual game, reinforces his premise that human existence is a compound of masks and illusions. The brothel is a violent and sordid place. Genet makes it a mirror of the world. Genet demanded that *The Balcony* be played not as a satire but as "the glorification of the Image and of the Reflection. Its meaning—satirical or not—will appear only in this case" (*OC,* 4:276). The brothel, with its hidden chambers, eroticized props, and illicit and illusory freedoms, is a magnificent metaphor for the unconscious as well as for society. Genet destroyed the mythical deposits grounding traditional Western societies and constructed his own (more honest ones, he would have claimed) from the remnants.

Too scandalous for the Paris stage in 1957, *The Balcony* had its premiere in London in a private club. It was performed in Berlin in 1959 and in New York in 1960, where it became a huge off-Broadway success. When Peter Brook was finally able to stage it in Paris in 1962, following a successful run there of the more scandalous *The Blacks,* it did not cause the expected furor. Jean-Jacques Gautier's denunciation of *The Balcony* as "delirious, nightmarish, lunatic, morbid, scandal-provoking," may have appealed more to Genet than Bernard Dort's comparison of it to Shakespeare and Calderón (Coe, 100). *The Balcony* has continued to challenge some of the most innovative directors of the contemporary theater.

Elle (She)

In 1955, just after completing a first version of *The Balcony,* Genet wrote a long one-act play, *Elle,* which he completed, except for one small section, and signed, but did not revise for publication. It was published posthumously in 1989. In *Elle* Genet again depicts the conflict between image and function, but in a much more playful, almost farcical vein. *Elle* brings together a photographer on a mission to take an official portrait of the pope, the pope's attendant, a cardinal sneaking off to go fishing, and finally the pope himself, on roller skates, who distresses the photographer with the progressive revelation that his existence is nothing more than theater. A "real" pope, he has no more substance behind the facade of his pomp and ceremonial robes than the fake bishop in *The Balcony:* "directed toward an image: magnetized by it. Alas, proportionately I lost all my interior density, and, outside of me, I watched an image dance."[12]

Les Nègres (The Blacks)

Genet wrote *The Blacks* in 1957 at the request of an actor who wanted a play for an all-black cast. Written for black performers, it requires a white audience. A prefatory note explains that if it is played for a black audience, a white person must be invited to each performance. If no white person accepts, white masks are to be distributed to the black spectators.[13] The black actors' performance, meant to alarm both the caricatural "whites" on stage and their mirror image on the other side of the footlights, is an even more elaborate experiment with a play within the play. The Pirandellian device is ideally suited to the situation of the blacks, whom Genet portrays as able to achieve authenticity only through a brazen exaggeration of the stereotypical roles the whites have created for them: "scarred, smelly, thick-lipped, snub-nosed Negro, an eater and guzzler of Whites and all other colors, a drooling, sweating, belching, spitting, coughing, farting goat-fucker, a licker of white boots, a good-for-nothing, sick, oozing oil and sweat, limp and submissive" (*Blacks,* 27).

From the opening moments, Genet implicates the spectators in a voyeuristic role by specifying that the curtains are to be drawn back, not raised, on a garishly lit stage where four Negro couples, minstrel parodies with faces made up with black shoe polish, dance to music by Mozart around a white-draped catafalque piled with flowers. At the foot of the catafalque lies the stereotypical shoe shine box. While they dance, a sumptuously dressed white court takes its place on one of the high platforms surrounding the stage. The court, composed of a queen, a missionary, a governor, and a valet, is played by black actors wearing masks of white faces, around which can be seen a ring of black skin. Seated on high, the white court mirrors the presumably white audience on the other side of the stage as they judge the black crime being performed before them.

With the arrival of the white court, the dancing stops. Archibald, the master of ceremonies, addressing in turn both court and spectators, assures the audience that there is no danger of the drama that is about to be presented "worming its way into your precious lives," because his actors will have the decency, learned from the whites, to make communication impossible (*Blacks,* 12). "Tonight," Archibald announces, pointing to the catafalque, "our sole concern will be to entertain you." The entertainment is a rape-murder of a white woman presented as a daily ritual scandalously charged with poetry and ferocious humor: "So we have killed this white woman. There she lies. . . . Only *we* could have done it the way we did it—savagely" (*Blacks,* 14). The ritual is one that cannot be changed, Archibald warns Village, the killer, "unless, of course, you hit upon some cruel detail that heightens it" (*Blacks,* 18). When the murder is re-enacted, Diouf, the curate, despised for being conciliatory, is made to put on a dress and play the role of a white woman whom the blacks assault with a litany of insults and obscenities. A white spectator is called up on stage to hold Diouf's knitting while he gives birth to large white dolls that duplicate the members of the court. After his "death," Diouf ascends to the platform occupied by the court, but the dolls remain on stage. Thus, even when the court figures later remove their masks, a symbolic white presence is maintained.

The second phase of the performance takes place in Africa. There is no scenery shift. When the frightened, drunken, belching court, staggering backward into Africa in imitation of its colonial predecessors, appears at stage level after a few minutes' absence, black Africa comes into existence in the sounds of the Negroes. Almost invisible under the balcony, they croak, hoot, hiss, and moan like the wind, creating the terrifying sounds of a virgin forest where all, in the words of the white Governor, "is leprosy, sorcery, danger, madness" (*Blacks,* 92). In this imaginary Africa, the whites and blacks confront each other for the first time on the same physical plane. The revolt shifts to a linguistic arena. "By stretching language," Archibald had predicted earlier, "we'll distort it sufficiently to wrap ourselves in it and hide, whereas the masters contract it" (*Blacks,* 27). The Queen, no longer dominating from the superior position of her balcony, and the black Felicity square off in a long, surrealistic verbal duel. The Queen's white imagery, the language of a "pale odorless race, race without animal odors, without the pestilence of our swamps," fades before Felicity's torrid African imagery and her poetic affirmation, laced with humor and vulgarity, of earthy black beauty and power.

Eager to bring judgment and apply such *Ubu*esque measures to the black culprits as "puncturing of the abdomen, adrift in the eternal snows of our unconquered glaciers, Corsican blunderbuss, brass-knuckles, the guillotine, shoelaces, the itch, epilepsy," the court discovers that it has been duped (*Blacks,* 101). The catafalque is empty. The ritual murder was a mockery performed to distract the Whites from a serious event, the trial by blacks of one of their own leaders that is taking place offstage. Firecrackers explode announcing the execution of the traitor. The court figures remove their masks and join the others in a discussion of the offstage revolt. Before the actors can exit, however, they are reminded that the ritual must be completed. The members of the court put on their masks again, are shot, and consigned to hell. Before she dies, the Queen warns that the whites will probably return to power: "We shall lie torpid in the earth like larvae or moles, and if some day . . . ten thousand years hence . . ." (*Blacks,* 126). The blacks' triumph is as illusory as the ritual murder. At the end of the play, a black backdrop is raised to reveal a white-draped catafalque exactly like the one at center stage in the beginning. The Blacks, who had left the stage, are once again dancing around it. The suggestion of an endlessly repeated performance undoes the apparent black victory. Just as the white court was offered a false murder, the white spectators, duped and insulted for the duration of the play, have been offered a false exorcism of their prejudices.

Coming to the stage at a time of struggle for independence in Africa, racial conflict in the United States, and the promotion of the values of *négritude* and *africanité* by Aimé Césaire and Léopold Senghor, Genet's play was seized upon as a political statement. Genet identified closely with the blacks. Describing his hatred for France, where as a child he had been made to feel an outcast, he told an interviewer: "Subsequently I could only join all those suppressed colored people who revolted against the whites. Against all whites. Perhaps I am a black man who happens to have white or pink skin. I don't know my family."[14] As always, however, his political views in *The Blacks* are problematical. Unlike the rebels in *The Balcony,* the blacks are united in their revolt, but it is a bond forged from pure hatred, something not easily sustained in victory. The fact that the new leader who emerges from the offstage conflict is described as a charmer with a deep, caressing voice promises little more than sham. Jeannette Laillou Savona makes a useful distinction when she assesses *The Blacks* as a successful psychological study of subconscious racist feelings but as an incomplete political statement.[15]

Genet subtitled *The Blacks* a "clownerie," a clown show. Like the jesters of old, the clowning blacks are able to deliver harsh truths from the safety of masks and costumes. Equally important to Genet, who had been dazzled in 1955 by the circuslike acting style in the Peking Opera, the stereotypes of the circus and minstrel shows lent themselves to the creation of magnificent poetry and stage effects. *The Blacks* can be compared to the poetry with which Césaire launched the *négritude* movement, a poetry described by André Breton as "taking the most discredited materials, among them daily squalor and constraints, and ultimately producing neither gold nor the philosopher's stone, but freedom itself."[16] It is a stage poetry, both physical and verbal, that mixes beauty, bestiality, and humor in the manner dreamed of by Artaud.

The Blacks was first performed in 1958 at a provincial dramatic festival. When Roger Blin directed its premier performance in Paris in 1959 by La Compagnie des Griots, a group of amateur black actors from Africa and the West Indies, it provoked an expectable gamut of reactions, disturbing not only those habitually offended by Genet but also more liberal audiences troubled by its joyous violence and the caricatural treatment of blacks as well as whites. Eugène Ionesco walked out. There was also much praise indicating a growing acceptance of Genet's work as a part of the French literary canon. "A baroque play, sometimes filthy, and sometimes sophisticated," wrote the critic for *Arts,* "but this savage, this outlaw, this Byron of low life, is our Byron and our brother" (Latour, 41).

Les Paravents (The Screens)

Genet's last play, *The Screens* (1958), is his most savage; it is also his most abandonedly lyrical, disconcertingly beautiful, and freely comic play. Its extremes of language encompass farting as a funeral rite, imitations of barking dogs and barnyard animals, and the kind of dreamy poetic raving and drawings usually associated with madmen or surrealism. "So I'm laughter planted on two big feet in the dead of night deep in the countryside," the mother of Saïd, the play's principal male figure, calls out as she runs after something invisible. "I want to be seen more clearly! (*With yellow chalk, she draws a crescent moon on the black screen. . . . To the moon.*) Hello! I'm laughter—not any laughter, but the kind that appears when all goes wrong. . . . It's the night of the nettles. . . . Through the lords of old, go back to the Fairy, back to the Virgin, I, I've known since childhood that I belong . . . to the nettle family. . . . their bushes were my cruelty, my hypocritical meanness that I kept, with one hand behind my back, in order to hurt the world!"[17] *The Screens* is full of jokes, laughter, and dancing, cruelty, poverty, and excrement. It is a gigantic work. Four levels of stage platforms are necessary to create the simultaneous events of 17 scenes, originally involving 98 characters. More than four hours are required to perform it.

The title comes from the multiple screens that constitute the principal element of the decor, perhaps the most extraordinary use of decor as stage language in all of the theater of the absurd. Some of the screens are created by the set designer. Others, mobile screens that the actors carry on- and offstage with them, are decorated spontaneously by the actors during the performance with drawings that both symbolize their affective state and create the play's shifting locales and dreamlike temporal settings. Translucent screens serve as entrances to the Kingdom of the Dead, where most of the characters find themselves at the end of the play. Roger Blin, who directed the first production, compared the screens to the ideograms of Asian theater and the placards in Elizabethan plays: "For Genet they constitute a declaration of antirealism."[18] *The Screens,* although it treats the very real conflict between Arabs and colonial powers, is as insistently illusional as any other of Genet's plays. Just as the judge's illusion in *The Balcony* required that the prostitute confess real crimes, Genet insisted that "near the screen there must always be at least one real object . . . the function of which is to establish a contrast between its own reality and the objects that are drawn" (*S,* 10). Genet called for garish makeup and outlandish, anachronistic costumes that would also function as decor: "The costumes will not clothe them; stage costumes are a means of show."[19]

The Screens' multiple intrigues and incidents defy summary. They have as their focus the effect on a poverty-stricken Algerian village of the struggle for independence from the French. The time frame spans the Arabs' early acts of sabotage against the colonists, warfare with the French, and the coming to terms with independence. The colonists and French army are represented by caricatural figures in elaborately anachronistic costumes. Capable of disgusting brutality, they are also comical in their perversions and narcissism. Like the figureheads in *The Balcony* and the white court in *The Blacks,* their power depends on the sham of postcard images and symbols. One of the landowners leaves an enormous white pigskin glove to keep watch over his workers. They also depend on the imposition of their rarified language. "We're the lords of language. To tamper with roses is to tamper with language" (*S,* 74). This strange prophetic claim is made by a planter oblivious to the individuality of his Arab employees but so passionately attached to his roses that he has hung them with bells to be able to recognize them individually at night. The Arabs burn his roses. For all their despicable traits, however, the European power figures are more nuanced than they were in *The Blacks.* When they die and pass through the transparent screens to the Kingdom of the Dead, they mingle easily with the Arabs.

In characteristic defiance of acceptable liberal postures, Genet makes the Arabs almost as reprehensible as the colonial intruders. They hound and betray each other and observe a hypocritical social hierarchy of their own in the midst of their squalor. Once they get the upper hand in the struggle, they too succumb to the deadly appeal of symbols and logic and begin "organizing for the aesthetics of decease." The only figures officially raised to "heroic" status by Genet are Saïd and his wife Leila, two destitute outcasts, neither of whom plays a positive role in the revolt. Saïd steals from the other Arabs, poisons their wells, and gives away their military secrets. He mutilates Leila, plucking out one of her eyes. Leila, so ugly that Saïd forbids her to remove her black hood, is determined to merit the "consideration and an empress's couch" due a traitor's wife. She wallows in abjectness, toughens herself with nettles, cultivates a sewer stench, and becomes a beggar and a thief. Saïd and Leila sound the depths of evil and poetry. Their personal revolt, a perverted reflection of the forces that drive the political revolt, is tempered, nonetheless, by a tenderness unique in Genet's theater. The romance of Saïd and Leila, a song that Ommu, an old village woman, imagines "carried at night from door to door by the severed heads of dogs," was for Roger Blin the "great discovery" of *The Screens:* "the love that makes use of the words of hate, the words of scorn. That's the real subject, and not politics or colonialism."[20] Toward the end of *The Screens,* Leila, dying, stands alone on a darkened stage regretting her lost eye, which makes it difficult to find her way to the Kingdom of the Dead. She addresses affectionately both her stink, her double, and her husband: "If I could at least pick up my eye and put it back. Or find another one, a blue one, or a pink one! But mine's lost. . . . Go away, stink! . . . Who told you to stand beside me? . . . Oh well, sit down there if you like, and don't move, sovereign. (*A pause.*) Saïd, my nice Saïd, you put my eye out and you did right. Two eyes, that was a bit too much . . . as for the rest, yes I know, I've got the itch and my thighs are full of scabs" (*S,* 156).

Saïd is eventually summoned to become the symbol of the new Arab order, which, as the Missionary warns his fellow Europeans, has "just deified abjection." Assuming "the power of lice" as a substitute for the ancestral and moral nobility vaunted by the defeated colonial powers, the villagers want to incorporate it into a symbol. Ommu tells Saïd, "We're embalming your sordidness, your shittiness" (*S,* 192). Saïd's fantasized apotheosis is treated comically. Laughing, he fancies his brow in the nebulae but worries about the location of his feet. One of the Arabs imagines Saïd's "voice a hundred thousand trumpets; his smell all the clouds." Saïd resists furiously, however, when he realizes that to become their symbol is "leaving me dead alive." Worse, Ommu adds in a humorously surrealistic salute typical of the language of *The Screens,* "It's neither dead nor alive! . . . all honor to sordidness! Storm the living! . . . Legion of Honor, a comma on the whitewash of latrines!" (*S,* 193). Neither Saïd nor Leila passes through the screens to the Kingdom of the Dead.

The political climate in the 1960s and 1970s created by the conflict in North Africa and the Vietnam War focused attention on *The Screens* as a protest play. Genet's theater resonates with such a profound sense of injustice that it speaks forcefully on behalf of the oppressed in any historical context. Nevertheless, although he is clearly sympathetic to the Arab's cause, he does not so much take sides in *The Screens* between the colonial powers and the Arabs as he does side with the main characters, particularly the women, because they are ostracized. Like the role playing in *Deathwatch* and *The Maids,* the rebellion in *The Balcony,* and the ritualized fake murder in *The Blacks,* the Arab revolt reflects the "disturbing theme of the double, the image, the counterpart, the enemy brother," described by Sartre. The magnification of Saïd, Leila, and Saïd's mother suggests that in *The Screens* Genet was still primarily concerned with the transformation of living functions into the deathlike immutability of poetry and myth. *The Screens,* he said, "was an homage to death through beauty. An attempt to transform fecal matter into something of beauty."[21]

The Screens could not be produced in France in the middle of the Algerian War. In 1961, three years after the play was completed, Jean-Louis Barrault made the courageous decision to stage it at the Odéon, under the direction of Roger Blin. Blin's production, the only one with which Genet was closely involved, was not politicized: "Language was given the primary place, and the spectators' eyes were offered a debauchery of images."[22] Barrault had arranged for special police protection, anticipating that the depiction of the French army would be inflammatory. There were demonstrations, and offended members of the National Assembly called for the suppression of the state subsidy for the Odéon. Most of the spectators, however, responded to the poetry of the spectacle, as engaged as was Blin by its surrealistic exploration of other realities. "What attaches me theatrically to this play," explained Blin, "is that it constitutes a truly antirealistic declaration in favor of a truth of another order, proving that everything can be dared and meaningful outside of realism. The value of *The Screens* is that the words are comic and the effect is tragic: it is a tragedy with the language of the burlesque."[23] *The Screens* is a play whose timeliness and power are undiminished, but one so costly and difficult to stage that it is rarely performed.

Flight

At the end of *The Screens,* the villagers speak of forcing Saïd into legend by turning him into a song. Genet must have been apprehensive that as a playwright he too was being compromised as legend. He wrote no more plays after *The Screens,* although he continued to write essays, film scenarios, and political articles, and, just before his death, completed another autobiographical work, *Un Captif amoureux* (A Captive in Love). He spent the last years of his life supporting radical causes, still seeking his double among rebels and outsiders. In 1968 he entered the United States illegally to condemn the war in Vietnam at the Democratic National Convention in Chicago. He became involved with the Black Panthers. At Yale University in 1970 he made a widely publicized May Day speech, violently denouncing the American government. He lent his support to the Red Army Faction in Germany and to the Palestinians. The public quickly attempted to fix Genet in another image, that of a political revolutionary. He resisted as adamantly as Saïd. Asked if he had become a revolutionary, he said no, explaining, "My situation is that of a vagabond."[24] Genet, who had been suffering from throat cancer, died in 1986.

In his life Genet was everywhere an awkward fit. The same is true of his theater. The work of a playwright who has been called a theologian[25] and whom Sartre called a saint meshes awkwardly with even so flexible a concept as the theater of the absurd. In common with the other absurdist playwrights, Genet uses the theater to launch an attack that is both highly abstract and intensely, disturbingly personal on a society that has made alienation and exile the norm, not an exception. His language and imagery are so fiercely savage, however, that he often seems closer to Rimbaud, Lautréamont, and Artaud than to Ionesco, Beckett, or Adamov, who masked more of their anger and pain with a playful, distancing irony. With a clear affinity to symbolism and surrealism, Genet's theater attempted a turning inside out of the psyche to reveal its shocking, hidden fund of eroticism and cruelty. Like Artaud, he held out the symbolic doubles and the savage, ritualized poetry of an oneiric stage as a key to more profound metaphoric truths than those offered by conventional psychological theater.

Genet's insistence on the falsity of the theater is characteristic of the theater of the absurd. His characters, like Beckett's, Ionesco's, and Adamov's, are alienated, marginal creatures for whom language and role playing are the only means of constructing a tenable "reality," but there is more magic in their verbal constructions. Language for Genet, as for the surrealists, was not necessarily a disaster. It was also a powerful alchemical medium. Genet's images are also more politically subversive than those of most of the absurdist theater. During the late 1960s and the 1970s, when younger audiences began to reject the theater of the absurd as unhealthily focused inward, Genet's plays reached their peak of popularity.

Chapter Seven
Fernando Arrabal

Many other writers, among them Boris Vian, Roland Dubillard, René de Obaldia, Robert Pinget, Romain Weingarten, Francis Billetdoux, Jean Vauthier, Georges Schéhadé, Marguerite Duras, and Fernando Arrabal, enriched the tradition of the French theater of the absurd. Suspicious of ordinary language and the conventional mechanisms of the theater, they also experimented with stage language created from sounds, rhythms, and visual effects and the powerful imagery of dark humor, madness, and dreams to create other versions of modern man caught in the absurdities of a sideshow existence. Most of them began writing about the same time as Beckett, Ionesco, Genet, and Adamov, or even earlier, but, with the exception of Vian, Duras, and Arrabal, remained relatively unknown even in France until the early 1970s. Only Arrabal and Duras have won broad international recognition.[1] Duras's connection to absurdist theater was brief and tenuous, although particularly noteworthy because hers was a rare feminine voice. Her name was associated with the theater of the absurd primarily because of *Le Square (The Square),* first performed in 1956, which she adapted from an earlier novel by the same name. *The Square,* which depicts a monotonous and deceptive wait for fulfillment by characters on the margins of society, who fill in the void of their existence with words, seemed very close to Beckett's theater. Duras's later plays were not representative of the theater of the absurd, however. Moreover, it is as a novelist that she is best known. Thus, among the "relief troops," as these playwrights were called by Geneviève Serreau, Arrabal stands out as the most important figure.[2] Arrabal, who was much younger than Beckett, Genet, Ionesco, and Adamov, made remarkable contributions to the absurdist theater in the 1950s and early 1960s and then took its experimental elements in new directions.

Arrabal used his theater to wreak vengeance on maternal, political, and religious authority. His early plays are peopled by small-time washouts, haunted by the specter of death, who operate just beyond the pale of reason and social order. Their dialogues are either childishly sparse and simplistic or wildly surrealistic excursions to the marvelous. Like so much of the absurdist theater, Arrabal's plays are circular, ceremonial structures. Attempting to remodel the world to the scale of their limited energy and understanding, his characters invent abusive, blasphemous games and rituals with deadly consequences. This is a theater intended to shock, and the shock, Arrabal said, "must be savage."[3] He refused to observe any social niceties on stage. His characters urinate and fornicate as naturally as they wish for a sardine sandwich or for a war to end because they are afraid to be soldiers. More shocking is their eroticized cruelty, ranging from all manner of betrayal and torture to incest and necrophilia. They have frequent and cheerful recourse to murder, even infanticide, as a source of short-term amusement or to facilitate petty thefts. Yet for all their vicious and grotesque behavior, these blithely immoral characters, unwittingly parodying canned bourgeois ethics and language, exude a humorous warmth and innocence. Their puerile ineptitude, dreamy confusion, endless games, and wordplay are rich sources of the subversive black comedy that characterizes the theater of the absurd.

Background

Arrabal was born in Melilla, Spanish Morocco, in 1932. When he was four, his father, a Republican sympathizer, was arrested by the Fascists and sentenced to death, but the sentence was commuted to 30 years' imprisonment in Spain. Arrabal's mother, from a conservative Catholic background and ashamed of her husband's politics, moved her family back to Spain and maintained the fiction of his death. It was not until Arrabal was 17 that he discovered his mother's betrayal. Of his father's fate he was able to learn only that he had gone mad in prison and had been transferred to a psychiatric hospital from which he reportedly disappeared. Arrabal, who had been almost pathologically attached to his mother, refused to speak to her for nearly five years, although he continued to live at home. During those years he nursed his sense of betrayal into a dramatic perspective similar to that of Genet: "I made betrayal the essential element of my life. . . . I was becoming . . . a playwright fascinated by this vital, visceral attitude that is betrayal, a thousand times more exciting for a man of the theater than a simple historical fact, which is not vital but accidental."[4]

In Spain the young Arrabal was ostracized as a foreigner and cruelly teased about his unusually short stature and large head. Harshly educated by the Escalopian fathers and then in a military academy, Arrabal rebelled by ignoring his studies and frequenting movie theaters where he discovered the Marx brothers, Charlie Chaplin, and Laurel and Hardy. The splayed boots placed outside a junked car in his play *The Car Cemetery,* like Estragon's boots in *Godot,* are a tribute to the powerful influence of the early comic cinema. During desultory law studies in Madrid, Arrabal discovered

Kafka and Dostoyevski, influences strongly reflected in his plays. His favorite author, according to Arrabal, has always been Lewis Carroll.

Arrabal wrote his first full-length play, *Picnic on the Battlefield,* an anti-war satire inspired by the Korean War, in 1952, at age 20. A year later he completed *The Tricycle,* which earned him a scholarship from the French government. When he arrived in Paris in 1955, seriously ill with tuberculosis, it was the beginning of a permanent exile. Jean-Marie Serreau, a director closely identified with the theater of the absurd, staged *Picnic on the Battlefield* in Paris in 1959. A prolific writer in both French and Spanish, Arrabal has since published novels, poetry, and film scenarios, in addition to several volumes of plays.

Early Theater: *El cimenterio de automóviles (The Car Cemetery)*

Arrabal often remarked that he is nearly always the principal character of his plays or, if not, that the main character is someone very close to him. "The young man that one finds in most of my plays," he explained, "and who is like the others or who imagines himself like the others, realizes suddenly that there is in him something that permanently differentiates him, against which he can do absolutely nothing. . . . He feels invested by a messianic task, which manifests itself to him rather than to others because he bears in himself all the sadness of the earth" (Chesneau and Berenguer, 24). In *The Car Cemetery* (1957), the most important play of Arrabal's early period, the character who "bears all the sadness of the earth" is a derelict, simple-minded, trumpet-playing Christ figure named Emanou. Trumpet in one hand, a sewing basket in the other, he mechanically repeats a painfully memorized rationale for being good, while his passion is played out in an automobile junkyard.

The junked cars, shells of the modern world's most prized symbol of freedom and status, are among the most effective settings in the theater of the absurd for the demise of human values. They are not a backdrop but an actual stage habitat, a combination boarding house, brothel, and bunker, that mirrors the degraded savagery of modern urban existence. When Victor Garcia staged *The Car Cemetery* in 1966, he did not emphasize the poverty of the setting but sought to create a "derisory image of our world . . . 'the church, home, the place where you make love, where you tear each other apart, the place where you live, in other words.'"[5] The rusted frames also provide grandstand seating from which their invisible inhabitants, like a derisory Greek chorus in this absurd tragedy with an oedipal subplot, point their impertinent spyglasses and comment upon the action.

Emanou, who is a petty thief and has even murdered a few people (but only "real bastards," he explains), is "crucified" because, against orders from an unspecified authority, he amuses the poor, knits them scarves, and feeds them with a loaf of bread and a tin of sardines. He is betrayed by his fellow musicians. After a frenetic pursuit, Emanou, no longer able to remember his set piece on being good, is captured. He is arrested by Tiossido, a caricatural athlete, and Lasca, his tyrannical elderly female trainer, who constantly circle through the action as part of their exercises, and whose authority is symbolized by the race number pinned to Tiossido's shirt. Lasca and Tiossido, figures representing both Fascist Spain and the inevitable Arrabalian oedipal tangle, have emerged from a night of lovemaking in one of the junked cars dressed in police uniforms. They beat Emanou senseless and wheel him away, crucified on the handlebars of a bicycle.

Car Cemetery ends with a role shift within a circular pattern that suggests an unending cycle of senseless abusive behavior. Dila, the wife of the car cemetery's manservant, who had given herself to Emanou with the kind of generous immorality typical of Arrabal's sympathetic characters, rings a bell to wake up the cars' inhabitants for another day. Tasca and Tiossido reenter, running. This time, however, it is an exhausted Tasca who wears the racer's number, while a tireless Tiossido runs along, fanatically forcing her pace. Emanou and Dila—her name translates ironically as "say it," in a play where words are absurd and derisive laughter and physical violence convey the only certain messages—represent the "little people" repeatedly crushed by fascist politics in Spain and, more generally, by the difficulty of existence in a dehumanized modern society.

Arrabal, who left his directors free with his texts to "unleash delirium," was remarkably well served by Victor Garcia, who helped make Arrabal famous with his 1966 production of *Car Cemetery* in Dijon in a large warehouse. In Garcia's production, eight garishly painted cars were suspended from the ceiling, welded together to permit the actors to move about. The spectators, battered by loud noises and klieg lights, were seated in revolving chairs placed in the middle of the action.

Panic Theater: *L'Architecte et l'Empereur d'Assyrie (The Architect and the Emperor of Assyria)*

Although the association of Arrabal's early plays with the theater of the absurd facilitated his acceptance as an avant-garde playwright in Paris,

Arrabal increasingly chafed at the connection: "I believe that my plays come from more savage horizons, less speculative, and target more exemplary ends . . . more spectacular, less satirical" (Schifres, 38). In the early 1960s he distanced himself from it with the creation of a "panic theater," a name chosen because it incorporates the notions of the prefix *pan-* ("all"), panic, and the monstrosity of Pan, the half-man, half-goat Greek god. The flamboyant ceremonial productions of Arrabal's panic theater reflect both his affinity for the baroque and the influence of the postwar surrealist movement with which he had recently become involved. He described his panic theater as a "rigorously ordered ceremony" incorporating "tragedy and Guignol, poetry and vulgarity, comedy and melodrama, love and eroticism, the happening and the theory of ensembles, bad taste and aesthetic refinement, the sacrilegious and the sacred, murder and the exaltation of life, the sordid and the sublime."[6] Arrabal's panic plays break from the despair over language characteristic of Adamov, Ionesco, and Beckett. They celebrate verbal chaos as a powerful transformer and enricher of reality. Visual effects take precedence, however, over the spoken word in the rituals and metamorphoses of his panic plays, which resemble hallucinatory canvases. Arrabal maintained that the surrealist painters influenced him more than the poets. He was also seduced by the paintings of Goya and Hieronymous Bosch, whose works he often incorporated into his staging.

The Architect and the Emperor of Assyria (1967), generally considered Arrabal's finest play, blends the alienation and unlikely savage tenderness of Arrabal's early works with his "panic" emphasis on the visually fantastic. Its two acts consist of a vertiginously inventive series of lessons, games, role-playing, and a trial, all entailing costume and character shifts of dizzying rapidity and formulated in comic layers of dreamlike wordplay and savage sounds. Isolated on an island, the Emperor, the sole survivor of a plane crash, and the Architect, a native endowed with eternal youth and magical powers over nature, are "panic" versions of Robinson Crusoe and Friday. The Emperor, who reveals himself at the end of the play to be a minor office employee and a chronic failure, has dazzled the Architect with tales of his power and a splendidly anachronistic oriental court. The Architect, after just two years as the Emperor's pupil, has acquired an extensive knowledge of the gadgets and rituals of civilization and has mastered the Emperor's language and outlook, learning, for example, to blaspheme with relish and to play at modern war. They are an absurdly mismatched, sadistically affectionate couple who entertain and delude each other with hallucinatory rituals, anecdotes, and reminiscences. Unlike most of the vaudevillesque routines in the theater of the absurd, however, the goal of their antics is not so much the filling of an existential void as psychoanalytic exploration. The Freudian talking cure becomes an acting cure, complete with an amazing range of costumes.

Terrified that the Architect has abandoned him, the Emperor copes by engaging in a solo routine that is both a vaudeville tour de force and a revelation of profound alienation. He builds a scarecrow, which he dresses in his Emperor's garments, then stands before his double playing the absent Architect and acting out all the conflicting personae buried in his own fertile psyche. He becomes a Carmelite nun and her confessor, then a doctor and a woman in labor. After an agonized labor, he pulls a baby girl from under his Carmelite robe. He is also briefly a Martian. In the middle of all this, he recounts a pinball game (lost, of course) where the stakes were the existence of God.

Act 2 begins with the Architect at a table miming the carving and ingestion of a gigantic creature. He transforms the table into a judge's bench and initiates the pivotal confrontation in the play, the Emperor's trial, a magnificent satire of justice, which leads to the act of cannibalism he has just mimed. The two characters take on the multiple roles of the accused, the judge, and a string of witnesses in another remarkable sequence of costume shifts, sex and species changes, accusations, and blasphemies. The Architect's performance as a German shepherd leads to the core of the Emperor's drama. The Emperor has killed his mother with a hammer and fed her body, bit by bit, to his dog. Condemned by the Architect/judge, he begs the Architect to eat him, a gruesome version of the sexual desire that moved Genet's characters to attempt to become the desired other through murder.[7] "I want to be you and me at the same time. You'll eat all of me, Architect, you understand?"[8] The Architect does the Emperor's bidding, cursing him for the toughness of his flesh and for abandoning the game and leaving him alone. The cannibalistic act is a complicated ritual that must be played for both humorous effect and pathos. As the Architect, who is wearing the Emperor's mother's clothes since that was the last role he played, consumes the Emperor, he also gives birth to him. He becomes the Emperor, speaking in an imperious tone and language, dreaming megalomaniac dreams, and simultaneously losing his own primitive magic powers. Finally the Architect, who has crawled under the table to look for the Emperor's last bone, emerges in the Emperor's costume. The play ends as it began. The noise of a crash and an explosion of light bring together once again the Emperor and the Architect, but the frightened savage is now the Emperor, and the Architect, in freshly ironed clothes, has become the "civilized" survivor of the plane crash.

The Architect and the Emperor join ranks with an extraordinary assemblage of modern Everyman figures in the theater of the absurd—Beckett's tramps, Ionesco's Bérengers, Adamov's Professor Taranne—who have so lost their bearings in the modern world that their identities have become essentially interchangeable. Jorge Lavelli, who staged *The Architect and the Emperor* in Paris in 1967, described its two protagonists as "linked by a permanent play of masks that makes of these two characters a kind of abridged version of humanity."[9] In language and style, *The Emperor and the Architect* resembles Genet's *The Blacks* and *The Screens.* In both Arrabal's and Genet's theater the combination of lyricism and comically morbid cruelty in the cathartic rituals stuns the spectator. Lavelli's ceremonial treatment of *The Architect and the Emperor* in 1967 was a triumph. Even critics who regretted Arrabal's excesses of sadomasochistic violence and blasphemy were won over by the poetry of the play. One went so far as to call it Arrabal's *Phèdre.*[10]

Protest Theater: *Et ils passèrent les menottes aux fleurs (And They Put Handcuffs on the Flowers)*

In July 1967 Arrabal was imprisoned for three weeks in Spain for signing one of his books with a blasphemous inscription. Outraged by his encounter with political prisoners left to rot in Franco's prisons as well as by his own treatment, he politicized his theater. The most important of Arrabal's protest plays is *And They Put Handcuffs on the Flowers* (1968), a title taken from a poem by Federico García Lorca, who was killed by Fascist partisans early in the Spanish Civil War. The action takes place in a Spanish prison cell, where three men have been held as political prisoners for over 20 years. In scenes that shift abruptly from stark realism to blasphemic dreams and erotic visions, Arrabal evokes the repressive hypocrisy of church and state in Franco's Spain.

Arrabal directed *Handcuffs* himself when it was first performed in Paris in 1969 and again in 1972 in New York. He forced the spectators to share the prisoners' circumstances by greeting them with loud noises suggestive of both sexual intercourse and torture. The spectators were blindfolded by the actors, separated from their companions, and then literally trapped in the production by the location of their seats, subject to abuse or cuddling by the actors. Arrabal urged the audience to stay after the performances in Paris, don monks' hoods, and tell criminal or obscene anecdotes from their own lives. Those who stayed on were treated with such brutality that the production, still playing to full houses, was shut down by a court action. The mixed reviews that greeted *Handcuffs* in both Paris and New York typify the violently opposed reactions that Arrabal's plays have nearly always provoked. In the 22 April 1972 *New York Times,* critic Clive Barnes wrote of its "power and its pain" and hailed it as "the work of a poet." Other critics condemned the excessive crudity and violence and accused Arrabal of simply trying to outdo the scandals of *Hair* and *Oh! Calcutta!*

Although none of Arrabal's subsequent plays was as successful as *Handcuffs,* he became one of the most performed playwrights in Europe in the 1970s. The nudity, sexual explicitness, obscenity, and physical brutality that characterize much of his later theater were very much in vogue at that time. In the long run, however, Arrabal's reputation will likely rest on his earlier depictions of empty adults tenaciously pursuing their savage and childlike hallucinatory pleasures in the face an implacably absurd world. *Picnic on the Battlefield,* his first play, is still his most performed.

Chapter Eight

New Directions

By the time Beckett and Ionesco were playing in the prestigious state-subsidized theaters of Paris, the experimental French theater was moving in new directions. As is inevitable with any successful revolution, the tenets of the theater of the absurd had become too familiar and too acceptable. A new wave of nontraditional texts, modes of production, and audience expectations had begun to pose an avant-garde challenge. One of the most conspicuous changes that was taking place was the emancipation of directors from the playwright's text. In the culmination of a process that had begun with Wagner's advocacy of total theater, directors began to conceive of themselves as independent dramatic architects. Directors especially, but actors as well, increasingly viewed the playwright's text as a springboard for their own creative vision and political interpretations. There was a growing tendency on the French stage to reinvent the classics, especially Shakespeare's plays, or to abandon plays altogether. Directors, many of them influenced by the experiments of Jerzy Grotowski's Polish Laboratory Theater, turned increasingly to events, ideas, or nondramatic texts as performance sources.

The new approach is well illustrated by Victor Garcia, a director for whom the theater is primarily a visual experience: "One must refuse this literary pretention of the writer, the hypocrisy of the rights of the author. Something that enters through one ear and goes out through the other, inviolate, doesn't interest me."[1] Garcia's style and philosophy are directly opposed to those of directors like Roger Blin, Jacques Mauclair, Nicolas Bataille, and Jean-Marie Serreau, who inaugurated the theater of the absurd. To the very end of his career, Blin, who died in 1984 at work on a Beckett production, insisted that the decor must not overwhelm the text: "One must always adapt to the writing of the text, respect its syntax. One must connect with the manner in which the author breathes his text."[2]

The changes in French theater in the late 1960s and 1970s also reflected a significant shift in political attitudes. As the despair and political apathy of the 1950s gave way to social and political activism in the 1960s, many of the premises of the absurdist theater, particularly its more neurotic underpinnings, were dismissed by a younger generation as narcissistic and unproductively nihilistic. Brechtian theater, which had been an important current on the French stage from the time of the first performances of Brecht's Berliner Ensemble in Paris in 1954, became all the more prevalent.

As it became politicized, theater also became more spontaneous and popular. Innovative acting companies took their radical views to the streets and to such nontraditional spaces as warehouses and factories. The French theater in the late 1960s and 1970s was heavily influenced by the improvisational "peoples' theater" that developed in the era of anti–Vietnam War protest and civil rights marches in the United States. Revolutionary groups like the Campesino Theater, a Chicano troupe formed during a long agricultural strike in California; the nonviolent Bread and Puppet Theater, which performed in the streets of New York with gigantic puppets; and The Living Theater were very successful when they toured in France. The founders of The Living Theater, Julian Beck and Judith Malvina, vociferously rejected conventional theaters as models of capitalist exploitation and turned their troupe into a communal enterprise and a voice for the radical left. It became a model for spontaneous experimental theater that, in the form of protests, happenings, and guerrilla theater, was becoming increasingly violent. The visual, verbal, and physical assaults that The Living Theater based on Artaud's concept of total theater were meant to shock audiences into antiestablishment political activism. Beck made the Artaudian claim that the infliction of pain on the spectator at a public ceremony could be a means to reconnecting him with his feelings and destroying his urge to violence.[3] Although in a different manner, the actors in Grotowski's theater also confronted the audience directly, often violently, forcing it to become a part of a production conceived as a process of "collective self-analysis" (Roose-Evans, 64). These confrontational, interactive techniques became an integral element of much of the postabsurdist experimental theater.

The occupation of the Odéon Theater in May 1968, a tribute to the power of the theater in France, even if for many an unwelcome one, was also an influential force in the evolution of the French stage. The debates that preceded the occupation made clear how alienated the young generation had become from even radical productions like *The Screens*. Among the reasons given by the young revolutionaries for attacking the Odéon was the fact that it presented leftist plays: "To play out the revolution on a stage, or to see it staged, is the best means to justify a nonrevolutionary attitude on the part of the public."[4] They called for a theater that would guarantee freedom and self-expression to everyone: "We no longer want a stage where a few individuals grimace and contort themselves for the amusement of a passive public ready to accept everything because it paid for its seats" (Ravignant, 42). Although the student revolt was quickly crushed by the French government in 1968, its dadaist slogans, such as "Art is dead! Let us create our daily lives!," and its festive, improvised performances inspired some of the most innovative productions of the 1970s.

The most successful example of the post-1968 theater in France was *1789, "The Revolution Must Continue to the Perfection of Happiness,"* performed by Ariane Mnouchkine's Théâtre du Soleil from 1971 to 1973 in an old cartridge factory in Vincennes, a suburb of Paris. Wanting a vehicle for protest against the French government, Mnouchkine's troupe chose the most familiar event of French history, the French Revolution, which they reinterpreted for the audience, after months of intensive research by the actors, in a series of 18 improvised episodes. *1789* broke down barriers not only for the actors, who improvised in groups and shared tasks from sweeping to costume making, but also for the audience. Before the performance, the audience mingled with the actors while they put on their costumes and makeup. There were no assigned seats. Spectators could sit in bleachers at one end of the acting space or stand in the middle of the performance, mingling with the wandering acrobats and participating in carnavalesque sideshows while they followed as they wished the simultaneously unfolding events.[5] David Bradby compares the effect of *1789* on the French theater of the 1970s to that of *Waiting for Godot* on the theater of the 1950s: "It established in the eye of the theatre-going public a new dramatic form, *la création collective,* and brought a flood of critical and explanatory writing in its wake" (Bradby, 195).

Although much of the experimental theater that followed the theater of the absurd was conceived as a determined rejection of the visions and methods of the absurdist playwrights and their directors, fertile ground had been broken for it by the theater of the absurd. For two decades plays of Beckett, Ionesco, Adamov, and Genet had revolutionized audience expectations by denying spectators a safe intellectual distance from the events of a play. Their insistence that theater is dramatic fiction rather than a forum for psychological case studies, not reality but another, potentially terrifyingly revelatory, way of looking at reality, had eliminated the safe pleasures of identification and catharsis and had forced audiences to consider theater as something other than an evening's diversion. By addressing the audience directly and often aggressively and insisting on its voyeurist role in the theater, the absurdists had forced their audience to acknowledge its involvement in the performance in an entirely new way.

The theater of the absurd had also prepared the way for the popularization of the theater in the 1960s and 1970s. It had broken down some of the formality of traditional theater by incorporating into its language and staging the rambunctious, irreverent physical and verbal tactics of the circus, vaudeville, and comic cinema. Highbrow, occasionally, in its poetry, it nevertheless humanized and demystified the theater by making the stage the domain of a series of bumbling, alienated Everymen who coped inadequately or not at all with a "civilization" that had reduced them to muddled inconsequence by destroying the communicative power of language.

Building on a rich heritage from Flaubert and the nineteenth-century *poètes maudits,* Wagner, Nietzsche, Jarry, expressionism, Dada, surrealism, and Artaud, the absurdist playwrights experimented with both the written word and the physical properties of the stage and renewed the theater with a new language of dreams, incoherence, silence, nonsense, light, sound, and gesture. Their successors carried on essentially the same kind of exploration, even though they tended to direct it to political rather than metaphysical ends and to concentrate on the spectacle and the performance, not the written text. When playwright Armand Gatti, one of the most creative and politically dedicated contributors to collective theater says, "Even my political stance is the search for language. For me looking for a language means looking for life," he is expressing the legacy of the theater of the absurd.[6]

The theater of the absurd, which emerged at midpoint in the twentieth century, may well be this century's crowning theatrical achievement. There were many remarkable productions in the 1970s and 1980s. As was true for most Dada and surrealist performances, however, the emphasis on decor and spontaneous creation over text makes them ultimately ephemeral unless reproduced on film. The absurdist playwrights were able to combine and capture the nihilistic irrationalism of Dada, the surrealists' poetic exploration of the unconscious, the metaphysical anguish of the existentialists, and the crumbling of literary, linguistic, and ideological havens in the aftermath of World War II in a form that is both solidly fixed in the poetry of the text and at the same time an invitation to revolutionary staging. The theatre of the absurd is an enduring challenge to the eye, the ear, and the mind.

Notes and References

Introduction

1. Martin Esslin, *The Theatre of the Absurd* (New York: Pelican Books, 1983), 26; hereafter cited in the text. Besides Pinter, among those writing in languages other than French who have since become well known are Vaclav Havel (Czech), Witold Gombrowicz (Polish), Tom Stoppard (British), Max Frisch (German-Swiss), Günter Grass (German), and the Americans Edward Albee, Sam Shepard, Jack Gelber, and Arthur L. Kopit. Other French-speaking absurdist playwrights are listed in chapter 9.

2. Antonin Artaud, *The Theater and Its Double,* trans. Mary Caroline Richards (New York: Grove Press, 1958), 37; hereafter cited in the text as *TD.*

3. Peter Brook, *The Empty Space* (New York: Atheneum, 1968), 53.

4. Arthur Adamov, *L'Aveu* (Paris: Sagittaire, 1946), 19, as quoted in Esslin, 93.

5. Samuel Beckett, *Waiting for Godot* (New York: Grove Press, 1954), 27; hereafter cited in the text as *G.*

6. As quoted in Geneviève Latour, ed., *Petites scènes, grand théâtre* (Paris: La Délégation à l'action artistique de la ville de Paris, 1986), 58; hereafter cited in the text.

7. Henri Peyre, *French Literary Imagination and Dostoevsky and Other Essays* (Tuscaloosa: University of Alabama Press, 1975), 63.

8. Eugène Ionesco, *Notes and Counter Notes,* trans. Donald Watson (New York: Grove Press, 1964), 157; hereafter cited in the text as *NCN.*

9. Albert Camus, *The Myth of Sisyphus and Other Essays* (New York: Random House, 1955), 90.

10. Jean-Paul Sartre, *What Is Literature?,* trans. Bernard Frechtman (New York: Harper & Row, 1965), 278–79.

11. In a 1937 letter to Axel Kahn quoted in S. E. Gontarski, ed., *On Beckett: Essays and Criticism* (New York: Grove Press, 1986), 5.

12. Esslin discusses these movements in a kind of posthistory of the theater of the absurd, a chapter entitled "The Tradition of the Absurd" (Esslin, 356–98).

Chapter One

1. Gustave Flaubert, *The Dictionary of Accepted Ideas, trans. and ed. Jacques Barzun (Norfolk, Conn.: New Directions, 1954), 3. Flaubert's Dictionnaire des idées reçues* was first published as a supplement to his *Bouvard et Pecuchet* in 1881.

2. In his introduction to Flaubert's *Dictionary of Accepted Ideas,* Jacques

Barzun describes a play written and circulated privately by Flaubert, entitled *Castle of the Hearts,* which is astonishingly similar to Ionesco's *The Bald Soprano.* In identical houses along a Paris street, identical bourgeois families eat identical meals, exchange identical words, and make identical gestures (Flaubert, *Dictionary,* 5).

3. Matei Calinescu, *Five Faces of Modernity* (Durham, N.C.: Duke University Press, 1987), 54–55.

4. Iris Murdoch, *Sartre: Romantic Rationalist* (New Haven, Conn.: Yale University Press, 1953), 29.

5. Le Comte de Lautréamont, Lautréamont's *Maldoror,* trans. Alexis Lykîard (London: Allison and Busby, 1983), 149.

6. As quoted in Gérard Damerval, *Ubu Roi: La Bombe comique de 1896* (Paris: Nizet, 1984), 13.

7. Roger Shattuck and Simon Watson Taylor, eds., *Selected Works of Alfred Jarry* (New York: Grove Press, 1965), 79; hereafter cited in the text as *SWAJ.*

8. Alfred Jarry, *Ubu Roi,* trans. Cyril Connolly and Simon Watson Taylor, in *The Ubu Plays* (New York: Grove Press, 1969), 72.

9. *Une Saison en enfer (A Season in Hell)* is the title Rimbaud gave to an 1873 collection of poems which includes his "Alchimie du verbe" ("Alchemy of the Word"), with the well-known line "In the end I found sacred the disorder of my mind."

9. Roger Shattuck, *The Banquet Years: The Arts in France, 1885–1918* (Freeport, N.Y.: Books for Libraries Press, 1972) 248.

10. André Breton, *Anthologie de l'humour noir* (Paris: Jean-Jacques Pauvert, 1966), 359.

11. Liam O'Leary, *The Silent Cinema* (London: Studio Vista; New York: Dutton, 1970), 11.

12. It has been estimated that by 1914 there were 60,000 movie theaters (O'Leary, 20).

13. Claude Schumacher, *Alfred Jarry and Guillaume Apollinaire* (New York: Grove Press, 1985), 142.

14. George E. Wellwarth and Michael Benedikt, eds., *Modern French Theatre: An Anthology of Plays* (New York: Dutton, 1966), 66; hereafter cited in the text as *MFT.*

15. From a purely theatrical perspective, Nietzsche's most influential notion was his promotion of the violently irrational rituals of antiquity as models for a genuinely liberating theater. Experimental theater since the turn of the century has tried by practically every means imaginable to incorporate this powerful creative frenzy into its performances.

17. Tristan Tzara, *Seven Dada Manifestos and Lampisteries,* trans. Barbara Wright (London: John Calder; New York: Riverrun Press, 1981), 35; hereafter cited in the text as *L.*

18. Tristan Tzara, *The First Celestial Adventures of Mr. Antipyrine, Fire Ex-*

tinguisher in Mel Gordon, ed., *Dada Performance* (New York: PAJ, 1987), 57; hereafter cited in the text as *DP.*

19. Described in Micheline Tison-Braun, *Dada et le surréalisme* (Paris: Bordas, 1973), 8.

20. *Antonin Artaud, Selected Writings,* ed. Susan Sontag, (New York: Farrar, Straus & Giroux, 1976), 142; hereafter cited in the text as *SW.*

21. André Breton, *Manifestoes of Surrealism,* trans. Richard Seaver and Helen R. Lane (Ann Arbor: University of Michigan Press, 1972), 34; hereafter cited in the text as *M.*

22. Breton and Soupault modeled the entire first scene of their *If You Please,* a 1919 experiment with automatic writing, on Ganser's syndrome.

23. Roger Vitrac, *Théâtre* (Paris: Gallimard, 1946), 16.

24. Henri Béhar, *Étude sur le théâtre dada et surréaliste* (Paris: Gallimard, 1967), 162.

25. Eric Sellin, "Surrealist Aesthetics and the Theatrical Event," *Books Abroad* 2 (1969):169–71.

Chapter Two

1. Michel Carrouges, *André Breton et les données fondamentales du surréalisme* (Paris: Gallimard, 1955), 139–40.

2. Antonin Artaud, *Collected Works* (London: Calder and Boyars, 1968–76), 3:93; hereafter cited in the text as *CW.*

3. Ronald Hayman, *Artaud and After* (Oxford: Oxford University Press), 104.

4. It is impossible to assess the exact degree and nature of Artaud's influence on the absurdist playwrights. Beckett, Ionesco, and Arrabal denied being directly influenced by him, but their lengthy stage directions, which are an integral part of the texts of their plays, suggest that they were very aware of the revolutionary approach to stage language taken by Artaud.

5. As quoted in Bettina Knapp, *Antonin Artaud: Man of Vision* (Chicago: Swallow Press, 1980), 188.

6. As quoted in Ruby Cohn, *From Desire to Godot* (Berkeley and Los Angeles: University of California Press, 1987), 59; hereafter cited in the text.

7. As quoted in Paule Thévenin, "1896–1948," *Cahiers de la Compagnie Madeleine Renaud-Jean-Louis Barrault* 22–23 (May 1958): 42.

Chapter Three

1. Samuel Beckett, *Happy Days* (New York: Grove Press, 1961), 28; hereafter cited in the text as *HD.*

2. Samuel Beckett, *Endgame* (New York: Grove Press, 1958), 18; hereafter cited in the text as *E.*

3. Samuel Beckett, *Proust* (New York: Grove Press, 1970), 48; hereafter cited in the text as *P.*

4. A. Alvarez, *Samuel Beckett* (New York: Viking Press, 1973), 11; hereafter cited in the text.

5. Deirdre Bair, *Samuel Beckett* (New York: Harcourt Brace Jovanovich, 1978), 3–4.

6. As quoted in Gontarski, 223.

7. Samuel Beckett, "Dante . . . Bruno . Vico . . Joyce," in *Disjecta: Miscellaneous Writings and a Dramatic Fragment,* ed. Ruby Cohn (New York: Grove Press, 1984), 31.

8. Quoted in Colin Duckworth, *Angels of Darkness: Dramatic Effect in Samuel Beckett with Special Reference to Eugène Ionesco* (London: Allen & Unwin, 1972), 17.

9. As quoted in Bair, 470.

10. Beckett wrote the play in French and later translated it himself into English.

11. As quoted in Enoch Brater, *Why Beckett?* (London: Thames & Hudson, 1989), 64.

12. Beckett originally imagined them as clowns; it was Blin who transformed them into tramps.

13. So have some critics. One of the most plausible arguments to this effect is made by Frederick Busi in *The Transformations of Godot* (Lexington: University Press of Kentucky, 1980); hereafter cited in the text.

14. Quoted in Walter D. Asmus, "Beckett Directs *Godot,*" in Gontarski, 283.

15. As quoted in Alvarez, 51.

16. Bert O. States, *The Shape of Paradox: An Essay on Waiting for Godot* (Berkeley and Los Angeles: University of California Press, 1978), 31; hereafter cited in the text.

17. Cited as part of a much longer list of interpretations in Ruby Cohn, *Back to Beckett* (Princeton, N.J.: Princeton University Press, 1973), 131–32; hereafter cited in the text.

18. Alan Schneider, "Working with Beckett," in Gontarski, 237.

19. "The names Nagg and Hamm pun on Noah and Ham of Genesis, who are also survivors of a world catastrophe, safe in their shelter" (Cohn, *Back to Beckett,* 298).

20. Herbert Blau, "Notes from the Underground: *Waiting for Godot* and *Endgame,*" in Gontarski, 273.

21. As quoted in Ruby Cohn, "Beckett Directs *Endgame* and *Krapp's Last Tape,*" in Gontarski, 299.

22. Hugh Kenner, *Samuel Beckett: A Critical Study* (Berkeley and Los Angeles: University of California Press, 1968), 155.

23. Quoted in Dougald McMillan and Martha Fehsenfeld, *Beckett in the*

Theatre, vol. 1 (London: John Calder; New York: Riverrun Press, 1988), 168; hereafter cited in the text.

24. Quoted in Beryl S. Fletcher and John Fletcher, *A Student's Guide to the Plays of Samuel Beckett* (London: Faber & Faber, 1978), 89; hereafter cited in the text.

25. Samuel Beckett, *Krapps Last Tape,* in *The Collected Shorter Plays of Samuel Beckett* (New York: Grove Press, 1984), 62; hereafter cited in text as *SP.*

26. Beckett's "Directors Notebook" for the production he directed in 1969 in Berlin refers to the recorder as an "agent of masturbation," and he made textual changes for that production to emphasize that notion. See McMillan and Fehsenfeld, 285.

27. Robert Brustein, "Krapp and a Little Claptrap," *New Republic* 143 (22 February 1960): 21–22, as quoted in Bair, 515.

28. B. Poirat-Delpech, *"Oh les beaux jours!" Le Monde,* 31 October 1963.

29. Ruby Cohn discusses Beckett's "lineage" in *From Desire to Godot,* 175–76.

30. Fernando Arrabal, "In Connection with Samuel Beckett," in John Calder, ed., *Beckett at 60* (London: Calder & Boyars, 1967), 88.

Chapter Four

1. Eugène Ionesco, *Present Past, Past Present,* trans. Helen R. Lane (New York: Grove Press, 1971), 168; hereafter cited in the text as *PP.*

2. The name of the award-winning scene designer Jacques Noël, whose drawing for a theater program is the frontispiece for this book, has become synonymous with the theater of the absurd. Noël designed sets for all of Ionesco's plays as well as for plays by Beckett, Adamov, Audiberti, Weingarten, Duras, Dubillard, and Obaldia.

3. Jacques Lemarchand, "Cet homme continuera à nous surprendre," in *Carrefour,* 4 March 1959.

4. Eugène Ionesco, *Découvertes* (Geneva: Skira, 1969), 84.

5. Eugène Ionesco, *Entre la vie et le rêve: Entretiens avec Claude Bonnefoy* (Paris: Belfond, 1977), 16; hereafter cited in the text as *VR.*

6. Eugène Ionesco, quoted in *L'Avant-scène théâtrale* 673/674 (July–September 1980): 131.

7. Eugène Ionesco, *Four Plays: The Bald Soprano, The Lesson, Jack or the Submission, The Chairs,* trans. Donald M. Allen (New York: Grove Press, 1958), 9; hereafter cited in the text as *FP.* According to Nicolas Bataille, when he asked Jacques Noël to create the decor, he made sure that he had not read the play and requested "a living room for *Hedda Gabler.*" Nicolas Bataille, "La Bataille de la Cantatrice," in *Cahiers des saisons* 15 (Winter 1952):247.

8. Ionesco owed the title of his first play to the kind of chance event promoted by Dada and surrealism. During a rehearsal, an actor's slip of the tongue

produced the appropriately absurd image which was then incorporated into the text.

9. George Wellwarth, "Ionesco's Theory of the Drama," in Moshe Lazar, ed., *The Dream and the Play: Ionesco's Theatrical Quest* (Malibu, Calif.: Undena, 1982), 34.

10. In the original version, the maid calms the professor's fears by offering him the protection of an armband with a swastikalike insignia. Ionesco eliminated this when the play was performed.

11. Claude Abastado, *Eugène Ionesco* (Paris: Bordas, 1971), 71.

12. Quoted in *Cahiers des saisons* 15:219.

13. Eugène Ionesco, *Three Plays: Amédée, The New Tenant, Victims of Duty,* trans. Donald Watson (New York: Grove Press, 1958), 119; hereafter cited in the text as *ATV.*

14. Ionesco's theater is frequently misogynous. Female characters are usually wives who revert to controlling mother figures. They can be shrewish or sympathetic, even alluring, but only exceptionally imaginative.

15. Eugène Ionesco, *Fragments of a Journal,* trans. Jean Stewart (New York: Grove Press, 1968), 17; hereafter cited in the text as *F.*

16. Eugène Ionesco, *The Killer and Other Plays,* trans. Donald Watson (New York: Grove Press, 1960), 150; hereafter cited in the text as *K.*

17. Paul Giannoli, "Les Colères d'Ionesco," *Candide,* 7 December 1961, 9.

18. Eugène Ionesco, *Rhinoceros and Other Plays,* trans. Derek Prouse (New York: Grove Press, 1960), 17–18; hereafter cited in the text as *R.*

19. As quoted by Claude Abastado in supplementary material to *Rhinocéros* (Paris: Éditions Bordas, 1970), 184.

20. Eugène Ionesco, *A Stroll in the Air* and *Frenzy for Two,* trans. Donald Watson (New York: Grove Press, 1965), 52; hereafter cited in the text as *S.*

21. In an interview in *Libération*, 26 May 1962.

22. Eugène Ionesco, *Exit the King,* trans. Donald Watson (New York: Grove Press, 1963), 24; hereafter cited in the text as *EK.*

23. Bérenger incarnates the anguish expressed by Ionesco at the end of his *Fragments of a Journal:* "It's not possible that there should be no beginning again. So many parts to be played! I shall become a seed once more, I shall be reborn. I shall have to start earlier. I shall have to love more, to love better, I shall have to breathe more deeply, more fiercely" (147).

24. When Jorge Lavelli revived *Exit the King* at the Odéon in 1976, he used a play of light on walls constructed of a deflatable material to give the impression of a slow demolition.

25. Described in Simone Benmussa, *Eugène Ionesco* (Paris: Séghers, 1966), 110.

26. Jacques Lemarchand, in *Le Figaro Littéraire,* 5 January 1963, 16.

27. Ronald Hayman, *Eugène Ionesco* (London: Heinemann, 1972), 3.

Ionesco had been a Transcendant Satrap in the College of Pataphysics founded by admirers of Jarry.

28. Eugène Ionesco, *Hunger and Thirst and Other Plays,* trans. Jean Stewart and John Russell (New York: Grove Press, 1969), 12.

29. Eugène Ionesco, *Macbett,* trans. Charles Marowitz (New York: Grove Press, 1973), 14–15.

30. Eugène Ionesco, *A Hell of a Mess,* trans. Donald Watson (New York: Grove Press, 1975), 151.

31. Eugène Ionesco, *Un Homme en question* (Paris: Gallimard, 1979), 9.

32. Eugène Ionesco, "Depuis dix ans je me bats contre l'esprit bourgeois et les tyrannies politiques," *Arts* 758 (20–26 January 1955):5.

Chapter Five

1. Arthur Adamov, *Ici et maintenant* (Paris: Gallimard, 1964), 17; hereafter cited in the text as *IM.*

2. As quoted in René Gaudy, *Arthur Adamov* (Paris: Stock, 1971), 51; hereafter cited in the text.

3. Eugène Ionesco, in the preface to Marie-Claude Hubert, *Langage et corps fantasmé dans le théâtre des années cinquante* (Paris: Librairie Jose Corti, 1987), 6.

4. Arthur Adamov, *L'Homme et l'enfant* (Paris: Gallimard, 1968), 19; hereafter cited in the text as *HE.*

5. Arthur Adamov, *August Strindberg, dramaturge* (Paris: L'Arché, 1955), 61–62; hereafter cited in the text as *AS.*

6. Lily, according to Adamov, has a "name which suits her, as it does every woman, a flighty name" (*Théâtre* [Paris: Gallimard, 1953–68], 1:9). She inaugurates a long list of pretty young female characters in his theater who, although they are selfish and quick to betray, are subject in the long run to the same degradation and defeat as the male characters.

7. Arthur Adamov, *Théâtre,* 1:17.

8. Arthur Adamov, *La Parodie, L'Invasion* (Paris: Charlot, 1950), 17.

9. Carlos Lynes, Jr., "Adamov or le sens littéral in the Theatre," *Yale French Studies* 14 (1954–55):52.

10. Arthur Adamov, *Professor Taranne,* trans. Peter Meyer, in *Two Plays* (London: John Calder, 1962), 17; hereafter cited in the text as *TP.*

11. Arthur Adamov, *Je . . . ils* (Paris: Gallimard, 1969), 115.

12. Arthur Adamov, *Ping-Pong,* trans. Richard Howard (New York: Grove Press, 1959), 143.

13. Pierre Mélèse, *Arthur Adamov* (Paris: Seghers, 1973), 85.

14. Roger Planchon, "Le Sens de la marche d'Adamov," in *Les Nouvelles littéraires* 2563 (16–23 December 1976):16.

15. Arthur Adamov, "The Endless Humiliation," trans. Richard Howard, *Evergreen Review* 2, No. 8 (1959):85.

Chapter Six

1. Jean Genet, *Oeuvres Complètes* (Paris: Gallimard, 1968) 4:269; hereafter cited in text as *OC*. Reference is made to this edition for texts that have not been translated into English.

2. In his foreword to Jean Genet's *The Thief's Journal,* trans. Bernard Frechtman (New York: Grove Press, 1964), 7.

3. Robert Brustein, "Antonin Artaud and Jean Genet," in *The Theatre of Revolt* (Boston: Little, Brown, 1964), 378.

4. As quoted in Bettina Knapp, *Off-Stage Voices: Interviews with Modern French Dramatists* (Troy, N.Y.: Whitston, 1975), 40.

5. Jean Genet, *The Maids* and *Deathwatch,* trans. Bernard Frechtman (New York: Grove Press, 1962), 104; hereafter cited in the text as *MD*.

6. Genet rewrote *Deathwatch* in 1985, substantially changing the plot and making Green Eyes, not LeFranc, the central character.

7. Quoted in Richard N. Coe, ed., *The Theater of Jean Genet: A Casebook* (New York: Grove Press, 1970), 69.

8. Jean Genet, "A Note on Theatre," *Tulane Drama Review* 7 (Spring 1963):38.

9. Jean Genet, *The Balcony,* trans. Bernard Frechtman (New York: Grove Press, 1966), 49; hereafter cited in the text as *B*.

10. According to Genet, his starting point was Franco's Spain, and Roger's castration the "symbol of all Republicans who have acknowledged their defeat," but that from that point on "my play went one way while Spain went another" (Coe, 91).

11. See, for example, Lucien Goldmann's "The Theater of Jean Genet," in Peter Brook and Joseph Halpern, eds., *Genet: A Collection of Critical Essays* (Englewood Cliffs, N.J.: Prentice-Hall, 1979), 31–46, and his "Genet's *The Balcony:* a Realist Play," *Praxis* 4, no. 2 (1978):123–31.

12. Jean Genet, *Elle* (Lyon: L'Arbalète, 1989), 60–61.

13. *The Blacks,* trans. Bernard Frechtman (New York: Grove Press, 1960), 5; hereafter cited in the text as *Blacks*.

14. Hubert Fichte, "Interview with Jean Genet," in Brook and Halpern, 180.

15. Jeannette Laillou Savona, *Jean Genet* (New York: Grove Press, 1984), 114.

16. In his preface to *Cahier d'un Retour au Pays Natal/Return to My Native Land* (Paris: Présence africaine, 1971), 18.

17. Jean Genet, *The Screens,* trans. Bernard Frechtman (New York: Grove Press, 1962), 112; hereafter cited in the text as *S*.

18. As quoted in Nicole Zand, "Entretiens avec Roger Blin à propos des *Paravents* de Jean Genet," *Le Monde,* 16 April 1961.

19. Jean Genet, *Reflections on the Theatre and Other Writings,* trans. Richard Seaver (London: Faber & Faber, 1972), 12.

20. As quoted in Bernard-Marie Koltès and François Regnault, *La Famille des Orties* (Nanterre: Éditions Nanterre/Amandiers, 1983), 21.

21. As quoted by Roger Blin in Knapp, *Off-Stage Voices,* 40.

22. Odette Aslan, *Jean Genet* (Paris: Séghers, 1973), 99.

23. Zand, *Le Monde* 16 April 1961.

24. As quoted in Michèle Manceau, "Jean Genet chez les Panthères Noires," *Nouvel Observateur,* 25 May 1970, 35.

25. Michel Corvin describes Genet as "first of all a theologian" in his *Le Théâtre nouveau en France* (Paris: Presses Universitaires de France, 1987), 63.

Chapter Seven

1. Boris Vian's *L'Équarrissage pour tous (The knacker's ABC)* and *Le Goûter des généraux (The generals' tea party),* condemnations of war as a monstrous infantilism, and his *Les Batisseurs d'empire* (The empire builders), a humorous but terrifying depiction of a world haunted by death, were among the most inventive plays in the "new theater" of the late 1940s and 1950s. Vian's promising career was cut short by his premature death in 1959.

2. Geneviève Serreau, *Histoire du théâtre nouveau* (Paris: Gallimard, 1966), 148–74. Martin Esslin discusses many of the same playwrights in "Parallels and Proselytes," in *The Theatre of the Absurd.*

3. Alain Schifres, *Entretiens avec Arrabal* (Paris: Éditions Pierre Belfond, 1969), 164; hereafter cited in the text.

4. As quoted in Albert Chesneau and Angel Berenguer, *Plaidoyer pour une différence* (Grenoble: Presses Universitaires de Grenoble, 1978), 12–13; hereafter cited in the text.

5. Odette Aslan, "*Le Cimetière des voitures:* Un spectacle de Victor Garcia à partir de quatre pièces d'Arrabal," in *Les Voies de la création théâtrale*, ed. Jean Jacquot (Paris: Éditions du Centre national de la recherche scientifique, 1970), 1:320.

6. Fernando Arrabal, *Théâtre* (Paris: Christian Bourgois, 1967), 5:8.

7. Arrabal translated three of Genet's plays into Spanish: *Deathwatch, The Maids,* and *The Balcony.*

8. Fernando Arrabal, *The Architect and the Emperor of Assyria,* trans. Everard d'Harnoncourt and Adele Shank (New York: Grove Press, 1969), 85.

9. As quoted in Bernard Gille, *Fernando Arrabal* (Paris: Seghers, 1970), 143.

10. The comparison to Racine's classic tragedy was made by Gilles Sandier in *Arts* (29 March 1967).

Chapter Eight

1. As quoted in Denis Bablet and Jean Jacquot, eds., *Les Voies de la création théâtrale* (Paris: CNRS, 1975), 4:294.

2. As quoted in Lynda Peskine, *Roger Blin: Souvenirs et propos* (Paris: Gallimard, 1986), 63.

3. James Roose-Evans, *Experimental Theatre from Stanislavsky to Today* (New York: Universe Books, 1970), 151; hereafter cited in the text.

4. As quoted in Patrick Ravignant, *La Prise de l'Odéon* (Paris: Stock, 1968), 39.

5. The description of *1789* is based on Lenora Champagne, "The Beach beneath the Paving Stones: May 1968 and the French Theater," in Josette Féral, ed., *Theater in France: Ten Years of Research,* Special issue, *Substance* 18/19 (1977): 59–71, and David Bradby, *Modern French Drama, 1940–1980* (Cambridge: Cambridge University Press, 1984), 191–99.

6. Armand Gatti, "Singing in the Brain; or, Gatti to the Second Power," an interview with Roger Bensky in Féral, 57.

Selected Bibliography

PRIMARY WORKS

This section contains only plays and other works that bear directly on the theater, and only readily available editions.

Arthur Adamov

Plays in French

La Parodie. L'Invasion. Paris: Charlot, 1950.
Théâtre. Vol. 1. *La Parodie. L'Invasion. La Grande et la Petite Manoeuvre. Le Professeur Taranne.* Paris: Gallimard, 1953, 1970.
________. Vol. 2. *Le Sens de la marche. Les Retrouvailles. Le Ping-Pong.* Paris: Gallimard, 1955.
________. Vol. 3. *Paolo Paoli. La Politique des restes. Sainte Europe.* Paris: Gallimard, 1966.
________. Vol. 4. *Le Printemps 71. M. le Modéré.* Paris: Gallimard, 1968.
Comme nous avons été. In *La Nouvelle Revue française* 1, no. 3 (1953):431–45.
Les Apolitiques. In *La Nouvelle Critique* 101 (December 1958):124–31.
Théâtre de société: Intimité. Je ne suis pas Française. La Complainte du ridicule. Paris: Les Editeurs Français Réunis, 1958.
Off Limits. Paris: Gallimard, 1969.
Si l'été revenait. Paris: Gallimard, 1970.
Le Professor Taranne. In *"Le Professor Taranne" and "Pique-Nique en campagne,"* edited by Peter Norrish. London: Routledge, Chapman and Hall, 1989.

English Translations

As We Were. Translated by Richard Howard. *Evergreen Review* 1, no. 4 (1957):64–95.
Paolo Paoli. Translated by Geoffrey Bereton. London: Calder, 1959.
Ping-Pong. Translated by Richard Howard. New York: Grove Press, 1959.
Two Plays: Professor Taranne and *Ping-Pong.* Translated by Peter Meyer and Derek Prouse. London: Calder, 1962.

Essays, Memoirs, Journals

L'Aveu. Paris: Éditions du Sagittaire, 1946. Translated by Richard Howard as "The Endless Humiliation." *Evergreen Review* 2, no. 8 (1959):64–95.

Auguste Strindberg. Paris: l'Arché, 1955, 1982.

L'Homme et l'enfant. Paris: Gallimard, 1958.

Ici et maintenant. Paris: Gallimard, 1964.

Je . . . ils. Paris: Gallimard, 1969.

Fernando Arrabal

Plays in French

Arrabal's plays have been published by Christian Bourgois in Paris in the fifteen-volume *Théâtre:*

Vol. 1. *Oraison. Les Deux Bourreaux. Fando et Lis. Le Cimetière des voitures*. 1968.

Vol. 2. *Guernica. Le Labyrinthe. Le Tricycle. Pique-nique en campagne. La Bicyclette du condamné*. 1968.

Vol. 3. *Le Grand Cérémonial. Cérémonie pour un noir assassiné*. 1969.

Vol. 4. *Le Lai de Barbaras. Concert dans un oeuf*. 1969.

Vol. 5. *Théâtre panique. La Communion solennelle. Les Amours impossibles. Une Chèvre sur un nuage. La Jeunesse illustrée. Dieu est-il devenu fou? Strip-tease de la jalousie. Les Quatre Cubes. L'Architecte et l'empereur d'Assyrie*. 1967.

Vol. 6. *Le Jardin des délices. Bestialité érotique. Une Tortue nommé Dostoievsky*. 1969.

Vol. 7. *Théâtre de guerilla. Et ils passèrent les menottes aux fleurs. L'Aurore rouge et noir*. 1969.

Vol. 8. *Ars amandi. Dieu tenté par les mathématiques*. 1970.

Vol. 9. *Le Ciel et la merde. La Grande Revue du XXe siècle*. 1972.

Vol. 10. *Bella Ciao. La Guerre de mille ans*. 1972.

Vol. 11. *La Tour de Babel. La Marche royale. Une Orange sur le mont de Vénus. La Gloire en images*. 1976.

Vol. 12. *Théâtre bouffe. Vole-moi un petit millard; Les Pastaga des loufs; ou, Ouverture orang-outan. Punk et Punk et Colégram*. 1978.

Vol. 13. *Mon doux royaume saccagé. Le Roi de Sodome. Le Ciel et la merde II*. 1981.

Vol. 14. *L'Extravagante réussite de Jésus-Christ, Karl Marx et William Shakespeare. Lève-toi et rêve*. 1982.

Vol. 15. *Les Délices de la chair. La Ville dont le prince était une princesse*. 1984.

Also published by Christian Bourgois: *Sur le fil; ou, La Ballade du train fantôme*. 1974.

Jeunes Barbares d'aujourd'hui. 1975.

English Translations

Plays. Vol. 1. *Orison. Fando et Lis. The Two Executioners. The Car Cemetery.* London: Calder and Boyars, 1960.

________. Vol. 2. *Guernica. The Labyrinth. The Tricycle. Picnic on the Battlefield. The Condemned Man's Bicycle.* London: Calder and Boyars, 1967.

________. Vol. 3. *The Architect and the Emperor of Assyria. The Grand Ceremonial. The Solemn Communion.* London: Calder and Boyars, 1970.

The Automobile Graveyard and *The Two Executioners.* Translated by Richard Howard. Grove Press, 1960.

Picnic on the Battlefield. Translated by James Hewitt. *Evergreen Review* 4, no. 15 (November-December 1960):76–90.

Solemn Communion. Striptease of Jealousy. Impossible Loves. Translated by Bettina Knapp. *The Drama Review* 13, no. 1 (Fall 1968):77–86.

Groupuscule of My Heart. Translated by Bettina Knapp. *The Drama Review* 13, no. 4 (Summer 1969):123–28.

Guernica and Other Plays: The Labyrinth. The Tricycle. Picnic on the Battlefield. Translated by Barbara Wright. New York: Grove Press, 1969.

The Architect and the Emperor. Translated by Everard d'Harnoncourt and Adele Shank. New York: Grove Press, 1969.

And They Put Handcuffs on the Flowers. Translated by Charles Marowitz. New York: Grove Press, 1973.

Garden of Delights. Translated by Helen Gary Bishop and Tom Bishop. New York: Grove Press, 1974.

Interviews

Chesneau, Albert, and Angel Berenguer. *Plaidoyer pour une différence.* Grenoble: Presses Universitaires de Grenoble, 1978.

Knapp, Bettina. *Off-Stage Voices: Interviews with Modern French Dramatists.* Troy, N.Y.: Whitston, 1975.

Schifres, Alain. *Entretiens avec Arrabal.* Paris: Editions Pierre Belfond, 1969.

Antonin Artaud

Plays and Writings on the Theater

Oeuvres complètes, 24 vols. Paris: Gallimard, 1976–88. Vol. 1–5 contain Artaud's plays and his most important writing on the theater. English translation: *Collected Works,* vols. 1–4. London: Calder and Boyars, 1968–76.

Selected Writings. Edited by Susan Sontag. Translated by Helen Weaver. New York: Farrar, Straus and Giroux, 1976. Includes *Jet of Blood,* but the translation is less true to Artaud's style than George E. Wellwarth's (see below). Sontag's introduction is an exceptionally perceptive analysis of Artaud's work.

The Theater and Its Double. Translated by Mary Caroline Richards. New York: Grove Press, 1958.

The Jet of Blood. Translated by George E. Wellwarth. In *Modern French Theatre: An Anthology of Plays,* edited and translated by Michael Benedikt and George E. Wellwarth. New York: Dutton, 1964.

The Cenci. Translated by Simon Watson Taylor. New York: Grove Press, 1970.

Samuel Beckett

Plays

Because the first versions of Beckett's plays were written sometimes in French, sometimes in English, separate listings are not given for French and English versions. Translators' names are given only for plays not translated by Beckett.

En attendant Godot. Paris: Editions de Minuit, 1952, 1963. *Waiting for Godot.* New York: Grove Press, 1954.

Fin de partie and *Acte sans paroles.* Paris: Éditions de Minuit, 1957, 1965. *Endgame* and *Act without Words.* New York: Grove Press, 1958.

All That Fall. New York: Grove Press, 1957. *Tous ceux qui tombent.* Translated by Robert Pinget and Samuel Beckett. Paris: Editions de Minuit, 1957, 1958.

Krapp's Last Tape. In *Krapp's Last Tape and Other Pieces.* New York: Grove Press, 1960. *La Dernière bande* translated by Pierre Leyris and Samuel Beckett. In *La Dernière Bande* and *Cendres.* Paris: Editions de Minuit, 1960, 1968.

Embers. In *Krapp's Last Tape and Other Pieces. Cendres* translated by Robert Pinget and Samuel Beckett. Paris: Editions de Minuit, 1960, 1968.

Happy Days. New York: Grove Press, 1961. *Oh les beaux jours.* Paris: Editions de Minuit, 1963, 1969.

Words and Music. In *Cascando and Other Short Dramatic Pieces.* New York: Grove Press, 1967. *Paroles et musique.* In *Comédie et actes divers.* Paris: Editions de Minuit, 1966, 1969.

Acte sans paroles. In *Comédie et actes divers.*

Play. In *Cascando and Other Short Dramatic Pieces. Comédie.* In *Comédie et actes divers.*

Eh Joe. In *Cascando and Other Short Dramatic Pieces. Dis Joe.* In *Comédie et actes divers.*

Come and Go. In *Cascando and Other Short Dramatic Pieces. Va et vient.* In *Comédie et Actes divers.*

Film. In *Cascando and Other Short Stories.* Reprinted in *Film.* New York: Grove Press, 1969.

Breath. In *Gambit* 4, no. 15 (1969):5–9. Reprinted in *First Love and Other Shorts.* New York: Grove Press, 1974.

Not I. In *First Love and Other Shorts. Pas moi.* Paris: Editions de Minuit, 1975.

Footfalls. In *Ends and Odds.* New York: Grove Press, 1976. *Pas.* Paris: Editions de Minuit, 1977.

That Time. In *Ends and Odds. Cette fois.* Paris: Editions de Minuit, 1978.

Radio I. In *Ends and Odds.*

Radio II. In *Ends and Odds. Pochade radiophonique.* In *Minuit* 16 (November 1975).

Theatre I. In *Ends and Odds. Fragment de théâtre.* In *Minuit* 8 (March 1974).

Theatre II. In *Ends and Odds.*

A Piece of Monologue. In *Rockaby and Other Short Pieces.* New York: Grove Press, 1981.

Ohio Impromptu. In *Rockaby and Other Short Pieces. Impromptu d'Ohio.* In *Berceuse and Impromptu d'Ohio.* Paris: Editions de Minuit, 1982.

Rockaby. In *Rockaby and Other Short Pieces. Berceuse.* In *Berceuse and Impromptu d'Ohio.*

Catastrophe. In *Solo and Catastrophe.* Paris: Editions de Minuit, 1982. *Catastrophe.* In *Three Plays: Ohio Impromptu, Catastrophe, What Where.* New York: Grove Press, 1983.

What Where. In *Three Plays.*

With the exception of *Waiting for Godot, Endgame,* and *Happy Days,* all Beckett's plays can be found in *Collected Shorter Plays* (New York: Grove Press; London: Faber and Faber, 1984).

Essays and Criticism

Disjeta. Edited by Ruby Cohn. New York: Grove Press, 1984. Contains most of Beckett's critical essays.

Proust. London: Chatto & Windus, 1931. Reprint. New York: Grove Press, 1957.

Jean Genet

Plays in French

Les Bonnes. Lyon: L'Arbalète, 1947. 2d ed., preceded by "Comment jouer *Les Bonnes,*" 1963.

Haute Surveillance. Paris: Gallimard, 1947. Rev. ed., 1965. 2d rev. ed., 1968. 3d rev. ed., 1988.
Le Balcon. Lyon: L'Arbalète, 1956. Rev. ed., 1960. Definitive ed., preceded by "Comment jouer *Le Balcon*," 1962.
Les Nègres. Lyon: L'Arbalète, 1958. 2d ed., preceded by "Pour jouer *Les Nègres*," 1964.
Les Paravents. Lyon: L'Arbalète, 1961.
Elle. Lyon: L'Arbalète, 1989.

English translations

The Balcony. Translated by Bernard Frechtman. New York: Grove Press, 1960.
The Maids and *Deathwatch*. Translated by Bernard Frechtman. New York: Grove Press, 1962.
The Blacks. Translated by Bernard Frechtman. New York: Grove Press, 1962.
The Screens. Translated by Bernard Frechtman. New York: Grove Press, 1962.

Essays

Lettres à Roger Blin. Paris: Gallimard, 1966. *Letters to Roger Blin: Reflections on the Theater*. Translated by Richard Seaver. New York: Grove Press, 1969.

Eugène Ionesco

Plays in French

Ionesco's plays have been published by Gallimard in Paris in the seven-volume *Théâtre*.
Vol. 1. *La Cantatrice chauve. La Leçon. Jacques ou La Soumission. Les Chaises. Victimes du devoir. Amédée; ou, Comment s'en débarasser*. 1954.
Vol. 2. *L'Impromptu d'Alma. Tueur sans gages. Le Nouveau Locataire. L'Avenir est dans les oeufs. Le Maître. La Jeune Fille à marier*. 1958.
Vol. 3. *Rhinocéros. Le Piéton de l'air. Délire à deux. Le Tableau. Scène á quatre. Les Salutations. La Colère*. 1963.
Vol. 4. *Le Roi se meurt. La Soif et la faim. La Lacune. Le Salon de l'automobile. L'Oeuf dur. Pour préparer un oeuf dur. Le Jeune Homme à marier. Apprendre à marcher*. 1966.
Vol. 5. *Jeux de massacre. Macbett. La Vase. Exercices de conversation et de diction française pour étudiants américains*. 1974.
Vol. 6. *L'Homme aux valises. Ce formidable bordel*. 1975.
Vol. 7. *Voyages chez les morts, thèmes et variations*. 1981.

English translations

Four Plays: The Bald Soprano. The Lesson. The Chairs. Jack or The Submission. Translated by Donald M. Allen. New York: Grove Press, 1958.

Three Plays: Amédée. The New Tenant. Victims of Duty. Translated by Donald Watson. New York: Grove Press, 1958.

The Killer and Other Plays: Improvisation, or The Shepherd's Chameleon. Maid to Marry. Translated by Donald Watson. New York: Grove Press, 1960.

Rhinoceros and Other Plays: The Leader. The Future Is in the Eggs, or It Takes All Sorts to Make a World. Translated by Derek Prouse. New York: Grove Press, 1960.

Exit the King. Translated by Donald Watson. New York: Grove Press, 1963.

Two Plays: A Stroll in the Air and *Frenzy for Two or More.* Translated by Donald Watson. New York: Grove Press, 1968.

Hunger and Thirst and Other Plays: The Picture. Anger. Salutations. Translated by Jean Stewart and John Russell. New York: Grove Press, 1969.

Macbett. Translated by Charles Marowitz. New York: Grove Press, 1973.

A Hell of a Mess. Translated by Donald Watson. New York: Grove Press, 1975.

The Killing Game. Translated by Helen Gary Bishop. New York: Grove Press, 1974.

Man with Bags. Translated by Israel Horowitz. New York: Grove Press, 1977.

Journeys among the Dead. Translated by Barbara Wright. New York: Riverrun Press, 1984.

Journals, Essays, Memoirs

Notes et contre-notes. Paris: Gallimard, 1962, 1970. *Notes and Counter Notes: Writings on the Theater.* Translated by Donald Watson. New York: Grove Press, 1964.

Journal en miettes. Paris: Mercure de France, 1967. *Fragments of a Journal.* Translated by Jean Pace. New York: Grove Press, 1968.

Présent passé, passé Présent. Paris: Mercure de France, 1968. *Present Past, Past Present.* Translated by Helen Lane. New York: Grove Press, 1971.

Découvertes. Paris: Skira, 1969.

Antidotes. Paris: Gallimard, 1977.

Interview

Entre la vie et le rêve: Entretiens avec Claude Bonnefoy. Paris: Belfond, 1966, 1977.

SECONDARY WORKS

Works Treating More than One Author

Aslan, Odette. *Roger Blin and Twentieth-Century Playwrights*, Translated by Ruby Cohn. Cambridge: Cambridge University Press, 1987. Extensive analyses of Genet and Beckett.

Bradby, David. *Modern French Drama, 1940–1980*. Cambridge: Cambridge University Press, 1984. Outstanding critical resource.

Cahiers de la Compagnie Madeleine Renaud–Jean-Louis Barrault 53 (February 1966). Special issue on Ionesco, Beckett, and Pinget.

Cohn, Ruby. *From Desire to Godot: Pocket Theatre of Postwar Paris*. Berkeley and Los Angeles: University of California Press, 1987. Well-documented critical study; includes chapters on Sartre, Artaud, Ionesco, Adamov, Genet, and Beckett.

Corwin, Michel. *Le Théâtre nouveau en France*. Paris: Presses Universitaires de France, 1963. Rev. ed., 1987. Brief but comprehensive study of playwrights and directors from the 1950s through the 1980s.

Dejean, Jean-Luc. *Le Théâtre français depuis 1945*. Surveys theater trends with brief descriptions of both major and minor playwrights.

Duvignaud, Jean, and **Jean Lagoutte.** *Le Théâtre contemporain: Culture et contre-culture*. Paris: Larousse, 1974. Informative sociological study of the major French playwrights and theater trends of the 1950s and 1960s.

Esslin, Martin. *The Theatre of the Absurd*. 3d ed. New York: Pelican Books, 1983. Updated version of the work that introduced the concept of the theater of the absurd.

Hassan, Ihab. *The Dismemberment of Orpheus*. Madison: University of Wisconsin Press, 1982. Excellent chapters on existentialism, Beckett, and Genet.

Hubert, Marie-Claude. *Langage et corps fantasmé dans le théâtre des années cinquante*. Paris: Librairie Jose Corti, 1987. Scholarly assessments of Ionesco, Beckett, and Adamov. Includes interviews with Ionesco and Jean-Louis Barrault.

Jacquart, Emanuel. *Le Théâtre de dérision*. Paris: Gallimard, 1974. Very helpful studies of Beckett, Ionesco, and Adamov.

Knapp, Bettina. *Off-Stage Voices: Interviews with Modern French Dramatists*. Troy, N.Y.: Whitston, 1975. Includes interviews with Blin and Arrabal.

Latour, Geneviève, ed. *Petites scènes, grand théâtre*. Paris: La Délégation à l'Action Artistique de la Ville de Paris, 1986. Invaluable collection of excerpts from interviews and newspaper reviews, 1944–60.

Norrish, Peter. *New Tragedy and Comedy in France, 1945–1970*. Totowa, N.J.: Barnes & Noble, 1988. Informative chapters on Sartre, Camus, Beckett, Ionesco, Adamov, Genet, and Arrabal.

Serreau, Geneviève. *Histoire du nouveau théâtre*. Paris: Gallimard, 1966. Valuable early study by someone well acquainted with the directors and playwrights.

Vernois, Paul, ed. *L'Onirisme et l'insolite dans le théâtre français contemporain.* Paris: Klinckseick, 1974. Includes discussion of Jarry, Ionesco, Beckett, Genet, and Artaud as well as of Schéhadé, Tardieu, de Obaldia, and Weingarten.

Arthur Adamov

Abirached, Robert, Ernstpeter Ruhe, and **Richard Schwaderer.** *Lectures d'Adamov.* Actes du colloque international Würzburg 1981. Tübingen: Gunter Narr Verlag; Paris: Editions Jean-Michel Place, 1982. Varied perspectives reflecting renewed interest in Adamov's theater.

Bradby, David. *Adamov: Research Bibliography and Checklist.* London: Grant and Cutler, 1975. Bibliography and major performances through 1973.

Chahine, Samia Assad, *Regards sur le théâtre d'Arthur Adamov.* Paris: Nizet, 1981. Well-documented study of Adamov's treatment of history, space, and characterization.

Gaudy, René. *Arthur Adamov.* Paris: Stock, 1971. Brief general study; includes essays by directors who worked with Adamov.

McCann, John J., *The Theater of Arthur Adamov.* North Carolina Studies in the Romance Languages and Literatures, no. 161. Chapel Hill: University of North Carolina Press, 1975. Well-done critical survey.

Mélèse, Pierre. *Adamov.* Paris: Séghers, 1973. Critical survey supplemented by interviews and excerpts from the press.

Les Nouvelles Littéraires 2563 (16–23 December 1976). Special issue on Adamov.

John H. Reilly, *Arthur Adamov.* Boston: Twayne Publishers, 1974. Detailed critical survey with extensive bibliography.

Fernando Arrabal

Arata, Luis Oscar. *The Festive Play of Fernando Arrabal.* Lexington: University Press of Kentucky, 1982. Informative study of play, ritual, and episodic structure.

Aslan, Odette. "*Le Cimetière des voitures,* un spectacle de Victor Garcia, à partir de quatre pièces d'Arrabal." In *Les Voies de la création,* vol. 1, edited by Jean Jacquot, 311–40. Paris: Editions du CRNS, 1970. Detailed production analysis.

Berenguer, Angel. *L'Exil et la cérémonie dans le premier théâtre d'Arrabal.* Paris: Union Générale d'Éditions, 1977. Sociohistorical analysis of plays, 1952–58.

Berenguer, Angel, and **Joan Berenguer,** eds. *Fernando Arrabal.* Madrid: Espiral/Fundamentos, 1979. Broad range of critical essays and an interview. French and Spanish bibliography.

Daetwyler, Jean-Jacques. *Arrabal.* Lausanne: L'Âge de l'homme, 1975. Well-documented thematic study.

Donahoe, Thomas John. *The Theater of Fernando Arrabal.* New York: New York University Press, 1980. An excellent thematic study.

Gilles, Bernard. *Arrabal.* Paris: Editions Séghers, 1970. Critical survey of Arrabal's work with performance data.

Raymond-Mundschau, Françoise. *Arrabal.* Paris: Editions Universitaires, 1972. Psychologically oriented criticism.

Orenstein, Gloria. *The Theater of the Marvelous.* New York: New York University Press, 1975. Includes an important chapter on Arrabal: "A Surrealist Theatrical Tractate: Fernando Arrabal."

Podol, Peter. *Fernando Arrabal.* Boston: Twayne Publishers, 1978. Well-documented critical survey with detailed bibliography.

Ruyter-Tognotti, Danièle de. *De la prison à l'exil.* Structural analysis of later plays.

Antonin Artaud

Cahiers de la Compagnie Madeleine Renaud–Jean-Louis Barrault 22–23 (May 1958). A special issue emphasizing Artaud's influence on contemporary theater.

Costich, Julia F. *Antonin Artaud.* Boston: Twayne Publishers, 1978. Critical survey of his work.

Bermel, Albert. *Artaud's Theatre of Cruelty.* New York: Taplinger, 1977. Helpful examination of Artaud's sources and influence.

Greene, Naomi. *Antonin Artaud: Poet without Words.* New York: Simon & Schuster, 1970. Biographical oriented study.

Hayman, Ronald. *Artaud and After.* Oxford: Oxford University Press, 1977. Detailed analysis of Artaud's work and influence. Extensive chronology and bibliography.

Knapp, Bettina. *Antonin Artaud: Man of Vision.* Chicago: Swallow Press, 1969. Excellent descriptions of Artaud's plays and theater productions.

Sellin, Eric. *The Dramatic Concepts of Antonin Artaud.* Chicago: University of Chicago Press, 1968. Important study of Artaud's sources and theories.

Virmaux, Alain, and **Odette Virmaux.** *Antonin Artaud, Qui êtes-vous?* Paris: La Manufacture, 1986. Critical study based on recent documents.

Samuel Beckett

Alvarez, A. *Samuel Beckett.* New York: Viking Press, 1973. Good critical survey.

Andonian, Cathleen Culotta. *Samuel Beckett: A Reference Guide.* Boston: G. K. Hall, 1989. Most recent annotated bibliography for Beckett. Indexed by theme as well as authors and titles.

Ben-Zvi, Linda. *Samuel Beckett.* Boston: Twayne Publishers, 1987. Thorough and up-to-date critical survey with detailed bibliography.

Brater, Enoch. *Beckett at 80/Beckett in Context.* New York: Oxford University Press, 1986. Broad range of essays on Beckett's theater.

________. *Why Beckett.* London: Thames and Hudson, 1989. Performance descriptions and extensive photo documentation.

Busi, Frederick. *The Transformations of Godot.* Lexington: University Press of Kentucky, 1980. Analyses influences on Beckett's theater.

Calder, John, ed. *Beckett at 60: A Festschrift.* London: Calder and Boyars, 1967. Includes essays by actors and directors who worked with Beckett.

Chabert, Pierre, ed. *Samuel Beckett.* A special unnumbered edition of *Revue d'Esthétique.* Paris: Privat, 1986. Excellent collection of essays on Beckett at work as a writer and director.

Cohn, Ruby. *Back to Beckett.* Princeton, N.J.: Princeton University Press, 1973. Vivid chronological study of Beckett's fiction and plays.

________, ed. *Casebook on Waiting for Godot.* New York: Grove Press, 1967. Includes interesting selection of play reviews.

________. *Just Play.* Princeton, N.J.: Princeton University Press, 1980. Detailed description of performances. First printing of Beckett's *Human Wishes.*

Duckworth, Colin. *Angels of Darkness: Dramatic Effect in Samuel Beckett with Special Reference to Eugène Ionesco.* London: Allen & Unwin, 1972. Comparative study; includes an interview with Beckett and a survey of audience reaction to *Endgame* and *Godot.*

Fletcher, John, and **Beryl S. Fletcher.** *A Student's Guide to the Plays of Samuel Beckett.* London: Faber & Faber, 1978. Invaluable comprehensive introductory resource.

Fletcher, John, and **John Spurling.** *Beckett: A Study of His Plays.* New York: Hill and Wang, 1972. In-depth critical survey.

Gontarski, S. E., ed. *On Beckett: Essays and Criticism.* New York: Grove Press, 1986. Broad range of critical assessments by outstanding scholars, directors, and actors.

Hayman, Ronald. *Samuel Beckett.* New York: Frederick Ungar, 1973. Discussion of the major plays, with production photographs.

Kenner, Hugh. *Samuel Beckett: A Critical Study.* Berkeley and Los Angeles: University of California Press, 1968. Chapter 4, "Life in the Box," is a perceptive analysis of *Godot* and *Endgame.*

Simon, Alfred. *Samuel Beckett.* Paris: Belfond, 1983. Well-documented critical survey of Beckett's work; includes a detailed chronology and an international bibliography.

States, Bert O. *The Shape of Paradox: An Essay on "Waiting for Godot."* Berkeley and Los Angeles: University of California Press, 1978. An examination of biblical and mythical themes.

Jean Genet

Brooks, Peter, and **Joseph Halpern**, eds. *Genet: A Collection of Critical Essays.* Englewood Cliffs, N.J.: Prentice-Hall, 1979. Essays from diverse perspectives. Also an interview with Genet.

Cetta, Lewis T. *Profane Play, Ritual, and Jean Genet.* Tuscaloosa: University of Alabama Press, 1974. Helpful background on myth and ritual.

Chauduri, Una. *No Man's Stage: A Study of Genet's Major Plays.* Ann Arbor: University of Michigan Press, 1986. Interesting thematic approach.

Coe, Richard N. *The Vision of Jean Genet.* New York: Grove Press, 1968. A thorough critical study.

———. *The Theater of Jean Genet: A Casebook.* New York: Grove Press, 1970. Interesting production background and broad range of perspectives.

Henning, Sylvie. *Genet's Ritual Play.* Amsterdam: Rodopi, 1981. Analysis of ritual theater in the context of *The Maids.*

Moraly, Jean-Bernard. *Jean Genet, la vie écrite.* Paris: La Differérence, 1988. Excellent, up-to-date biographical study dispelling some of the Sartrian myths.

Oswald, Laura. *Jean Genet and the Semiotics of Performance.* Bloomington: Indiana University Press, 1989. Emphasizes continuity from novels to theater.

Sartre, Jean-Paul. *Saint Genet: Actor and Martyr.* Translated by Bernard Frechtman. New York: George Braziller, 1963. Existentialist critique of Genet's life and early writing; enormous influence on subsequent critical studies. Fascinating analysis of *The Maids.*

Savona, Jeanette L., *Jean Genet* (New York: Grove Press, 1983. Well done survey of Genet's Theater with emphasis on social and political themes.

Thody, Phillip. *Jean Genet: A Study of His Novels and Plays.* New York: Stein & Day, 1969. Thorough critical review.

Tulane Drama Review 7 (Spring 1963). Special issue on Genet and Ionesco.

Webb, Richard C., and **Suzanne A. Webb.** *Jean Genet and His Critics: An Annotated Bibliography, 1943–1980.* Methuen, N.J.: Scarecrow, 1982. An essential resource.

Eugène Ionesco

Abastado, Claude. *Eugène Ionesco.* Paris: Bordas, 1971. Thorough critical survey. Includes excerpts from the press and an interview with Ionesco.

Benmussa, Simone. *Ionesco.* Paris: Editors Séghers, 1966. Excellent analysis of early plays with emphasis on performance.

Cahiers de la Compagnie. Madeleine Renaud–Jean-Louis Barrault 29 (February, 1960). Special issue on *Rhinocéros.*

Cahiers des Saisons 15 (Winter 1959). Special issue on Ionesco.

Coe, Richard N. *Ionesco: A Study of His Plays.* London: Methuen, 1971. One of the best general works on Ionesco. Extensive bibliography and production data.

Duckworth, Colin. See entry for Beckett.

Ionesco: Situation et Perspectives. Paris: Pierre Belfond, 1980. Reproduces presentations at a 1978 colloquium on Ionesco at Cérisy-la-Salle; preface by Ionesco.

Lazar, Moshe, ed. *The Dream and the Play: Ionesco's Theatrical Quest.* Malibu, Calif.: Undena, 1982. A good collection of critical essays.

L'Avant-scène théâtrale, 1–15 February 1967, 373–74. Special issue on Ionesco.

Hayman, Ronald. *Eugene Ionesco.* New York: Frederick Ungar, 1976. A thorough critical study. Includes an interview with Ionesco.

Lamont, Rosette C. *Ionesco: A Collection of Critical Essays.* Englewood Cliffs, N.J.: Prentice-Hall, 1973. Broad range of interesting essays.

Tulane Drama Review 7 (Spring 1963). Special issue on Genet and Ionesco.

Vernois, Paul. *La Dynamique théâtrale d'Ionesco.* Paris: Editions Klincksieck, 1972. Scholarly thematic study.

Index

The Author

Deborah Gaensbauer is a professor of modern languages at Regis College, Denver, Colorado. Her articles on Eugène Ionesco, Marguerite Duras, and Virginia Woolf have appeared in *Modern Drama,* the *French Review,* and *Comparative Literature Studies.*

The Editor

David O'Connell is professor of foreign languages and chair of the Department of Foreign Languages at Georgia State University. He received his Ph.D. from Princeton University in 1966, where he was a National Woodrow Wilson Fellow, the Bergen Fellow in Romance Languages, and a National Woodrow Wilson Dissertation Fellow. He is the author of *The Teachings of Saint Louis: A Critical Text* (1972), *Les Propos de Saint Louis* (1974), *Louis-Ferdinand Céline* (1976), *The Instructions of Saint Louis: A Critical Text* (1979), and *Michel de Saint Pierre: A Catholic Novelist at the Crossroads* (1990). He is the editor of *Catholic Writers in France since 1945* (1983) and has served as review editor (1977–79) and Managing editor (1987–90) of the *French Review.*